Green Giant®

75th Anniversary

Making Meals Easy

with goodness from the valley

The Green Giant Company, a division of The Pillsbury Company

Making Meals Easy

Pillsbury Publications
The Pillsbury Company

Publisher: Sally Peters
Associate Publisher: Diane B. Anderson
Senior Food Editor: Andi Bidwell, C.C.P.
Project Manager: Marilyn French
Recipe Editor: Nancy A. Lilleberg
Contributing Writers: Mary Caldwell, Maggie Gilbert, Carrie Myers
Photography: Creative Publishing international, Graham Brown Photography, Tad Ware Photography
Food Stylists: Susan Brosious, JoAnn Cherry, Bobbette Destiche, Sharon Harding, Cindy Ojczyk, Barb Standal
Photo Coordinator: Karen Goodsell
Nutrition Information: Margaret Reinhardt, M.P.H., L.N., Gayle Smith
Recipe Typists: Renee Axtell, Lisa Moore, Mary Prokott

For more Green Giant recipes and food information, visit our web site at http://www.greengiant.com

Frontispiece Photo: Teriyaki Chicken with Ramen Noodles, page 38.

Creative Publishing international
Minnetonka, Minnesota 55343

President/CEO: David Murphy
Vice President, Custom Services: Sue Riley
Director, Custom Publishing: Hugh Kennedy
Account Manager: Marie Kruegel
Design Director: Jann Williams
Art Director: Jim Oldsberg
Copy Editor: Sandra Granseth
Photographer: Chuck Nields
Prop Stylist: Coralie Sathre
Studio Services Manager: Marcia Chambers
Project Manager: John Fletcher
Traffic Manager: Pete Skophammer
Production Manager: Janell Schmidt

Printed by R. R. Donnelley & Sons Co. USA

ISBN: 0-86573-169-1

Introduction

Let the celebration begin! This year marks our 75th anniversary of providing you with the best quality in packaged vegetables. When the Green Giant Company first started as a sweet corn cannery in Minnesota, we wanted to make sure that home cooks were getting all the flavor and nutrition that only fresh vegetables can bring to mealtimes. Since then, we believe we've kept that promise by continuing to create fresh, wholesome products that help today's families meet the needs of their dynamic schedules.

The Jolly Green Giant has been and always will be synonymous with freshness, quality and "good things from the Valley." We like to think of him as Mom's dinnertime ally in making family meals easy, fun and wholesome.

We know the importance of bringing the freshness of our vegetables into fast and easy mealtime recipes. We created this recipe book to provide you with a variety of flavorful meal suggestions from across the globe. There is a great selection of salads, appetizers, main courses and side dishes—from Hurry-Curry Corn Salad to Apricot Beef Stir-Fry to Easy Nacho Skillet Dinner—all to meet your cooking needs. Look for special ribbons marking Bake-Off® recipes and the Giant's Picks, favorite selections "from the Valley."

We hope you enjoy the recipes in this book and continue to look to Green Giant® products for innovative food ideas.

The Green Giant Company

Contents

Broccoli Cheddar Salad, pg. 8

APPETIZERS & SALADS

CHILI, SOUPS & STEWS

Italian Pasta and Veggie Soup, pg. 22

SKILLET DINNERS

Teriyaki Chicken with Ramen Noodles, pg. 38

CASEROLES

Mexican Spinach Casserole, pg. 66

SIDE DISHES

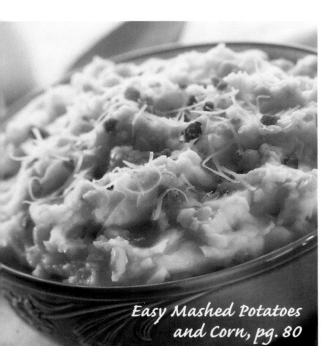

Easy Mashed Potatoes and Corn, pg. 80

Appetizers & Salads

Choose one of these hot or cold starters and begin your meal with a winner! Look for the "Bake-Off® Recipe" banner sprinkled throughout this collection of favorite vegetable dips, salads and hors d'oeuvres.

Broccoli Cheddar Salad
(page 8)

Broccoli Cheddar Salad

PICTURED ON PAGES 6–7
PREP TIME: 15 MINUTES

1 (14-OZ.) PKG. GREEN GIANT SELECT® FROZEN 100% BROCCOLI FLORETS

½ CUP PURCHASED RANCH SALAD DRESSING

2 OZ. (½ CUP) SHREDDED CHEDDAR CHEESE

2 TABLESPOONS REAL BACON BITS

2 TABLESPOONS SUNFLOWER SEEDS

(1) Cook broccoli as directed on package. Drain; cool.

(2) In medium bowl, combine broccoli and all remaining ingredients; toss to mix. Serve immediately, or cover and refrigerate until serving time.

Yield: 7 (½-cup) servings

NUTRITION INFORMATION: SERVING SIZE: ½ CUP
CALORIES 170 (82% FROM FAT) • FAT 15 G (SAT. 4 G) • CHOLESTEROL 15 MG
SODIUM 310 MG • CARBOHYDRATE 4 G • FIBER 2 G • PROTEIN 5 G

Bean and Corn Salsa

PREP TIME: 10 MINUTES

1 (15-OZ.) CAN BLACK BEANS, DRAINED, RINSED

1 (11-OZ.) CAN GREEN GIANT® NIBLETS® CORN, DRAINED

1 CUP CHOPPED TOMATOES OR 1 (14.5-OZ.) CAN DICED TOMATOES, DRAINED

½ CUP CHOPPED GREEN ONIONS

2 TABLESPOONS CHOPPED FRESH CILANTRO

½ CUP PURCHASED ITALIAN SALAD DRESSING

2 SERRANO CHILES, SEEDED, CHOPPED, IF DESIRED*

(1) In large bowl, combine all ingredients; mix well. Serve immediately, or cover and refrigerate until serving time. Serve with tortilla chips or over grilled meat.

Yield: 4 cups

TIP: * WHEN HANDLING FRESH SERRANO CHILES, WEAR PLASTIC OR RUBBER GLOVES TO PROTECT HANDS. DO NOT TOUCH FACE OR EYES.

NUTRITION INFORMATION: SERVING SIZE: ¼ CUP
CALORIES 80 (44% FROM FAT) • FAT 4 G (SAT. 1 G) • CHOLESTEROL 0 MG
SODIUM 170 MG • CARBOHYDRATE 9 G • FIBER 2 G • PROTEIN 2 G

Quick Spinach Dip

PREP TIME: 10 MINUTES (READY IN 3 HOURS 10 MINUTES)

1 (9-OZ.) PKG. GREEN GIANT® FROZEN SPINACH

1 (8-OZ.) CONTAINER CREAM CHEESE WITH CHIVES AND ONION

¾ CUP MAYONNAISE

1. Cook spinach as directed on package. Cool slightly. Squeeze to drain well.

2. In medium bowl, combine spinach and cream cheese; mix well. Fold in mayonnaise. Refrigerate at least 3 hours to blend flavors. Serve with cut-up fresh vegetables or assorted crackers.

Yield: 2¼ cups

NUTRITION INFORMATION: SERVING SIZE: 1 TABLESPOON CALORIES 60 (83% FROM FAT) • FAT 6 G (SAT. 2 G) • CHOLESTEROL 10 MG SODIUM 60 MG • CARBOHYDRATE 1 G • FIBER 0 G • PROTEIN 1 G

Baked Artichoke Squares

PREP TIME: 15 MINUTES (READY IN 35 MINUTES)

2 (8-OZ.) CANS PILLSBURY REFRIGERATED CRESCENT DINNER ROLLS

1 (14-OZ.) CAN ARTICHOKE HEARTS, DRAINED, CHOPPED

1 (9-OZ.) PKG. GREEN GIANT® FROZEN SPINACH, THAWED, SQUEEZED TO DRAIN

¾ CUP GRATED PARMESAN CHEESE

⅔ CUP MAYONNAISE

⅔ CUP SOUR CREAM

⅛ TEASPOON GARLIC POWDER

1. Heat oven to 375° F. Unroll dough into 4 long rectangles. Place crosswise in ungreased 15×10×1-inch baking pan; press over bottom and 1 inch up sides to form crust. Press perforations to seal.

2. Bake at 375° F. for 10 to 12 minutes or until light golden brown.

3. Meanwhile, in medium bowl, combine all remaining ingredients; mix well. Spread mixture evenly over partially baked crust.

4. Bake at 375° F. for an additional 8 to 10 minutes or until topping is thoroughly heated. Cut into about 1½-inch squares. Serve warm.

Yield: 60 appetizers

NUTRITION INFORMATION: SERVING SIZE: 1 APPETIZER CALORIES 60 (58% FROM FAT) • FAT 4 G (SAT. 1 G) • CHOLESTEROL 4 MG SODIUM 110 MG • CARBOHYDRATE 4 G • FIBER 0 G • PROTEIN 1 G

Creamy Spinach-Artichoke Dip

PREP TIME: 10 MINUTES (READY IN 35 MINUTES)

1 (14-OZ.) CAN ARTICHOKE HEARTS, DRAINED, CHOPPED
1 (9-OZ.) PKG. GREEN GIANT® FROZEN SPINACH, THAWED, SQUEEZED TO DRAIN
4 OZ. (1 CUP) SHREDDED MOZZARELLA CHEESE
½ CUP GRATED PARMESAN CHEESE
½ CUP MAYONNAISE
1 GARLIC CLOVE, MINCED
PAPRIKA

① Heat oven to 325° F. In 1-quart casserole, combine all ingredients except paprika; mix well. Sprinkle with paprika.

② Bake at 325° F. for 20 to 25 minutes or until bubbly and golden brown.

③ Serve with assorted crackers or cut-up fresh vegetables.

Yield: 2½ cups

NUTRITION INFORMATION: SERVING SIZE: 1 TABLESPOON
CALORIES 40 (63% FROM FAT) • FAT 3 G (SAT. 1 G) • CHOLESTEROL 4 MG
SODIUM 75 MG • CARBOHYDRATE 1 G • FIBER 0 G • PROTEIN 2 G

Easy Hot Spinach Dip

GIANT'S PICK

PREP TIME: 10 MINUTES

1 (9-OZ.) PKG. GREEN GIANT® FROZEN SPINACH
½ CUP SOUR CREAM
½ CUP MAYONNAISE
1 (5.2-OZ.) PKG. BOURSIN CHEESE
RED BELL PEPPER STRIPS, IF DESIRED

① Cook spinach as directed on package. Cool slightly. Squeeze to drain well.

② In microwave-safe bowl, combine sour cream, mayonnaise and cheese; mix well. Stir in spinach. Microwave on HIGH for 1 to 2 minutes or until thoroughly heated, stirring once during cooking. Garnish with red pepper strips. Serve with cut-up fresh vegetables or assorted crackers.

Yield: 2 cups

NUTRITION INFORMATION: SERVING SIZE: 1 TABLESPOON
CALORIES 50 (90% FROM FAT) • FAT 5 G (SAT. 2 G) • CHOLESTEROL 10 MG
SODIUM 70 MG • CARBOHYDRATE 1 G • FIBER 0 G • PROTEIN 1 G

Top: Creamy Spinach-Artichoke Dip •
Bottom: Easy Hot Spinach Dip

Hearty Spinach Braid

BAKE-OFF® RECIPE

PREP TIME: 15 MINUTES (READY IN 45 MINUTES)

1 (4.25-OZ.) CAN DEVILED HAM
OR CHICKEN SPREAD

2 EGGS

2 OZ. (½ CUP) SHREDDED SHARP
CHEDDAR CHEESE

1 SMALL SHALLOT, MINCED
DASH SALT, IF DESIRED

⅛ TEASPOON CRACKED BLACK PEPPER

1 (9-OZ.) PKG. GREEN GIANT® FROZEN
SPINACH, THAWED, SQUEEZED
TO DRAIN

1 (10-OZ.) CAN PILLSBURY REFRIGERATED
PIZZA CRUST

1 TEASPOON WATER

① Heat oven to 375° F. In medium bowl, combine deviled ham and 1 of the eggs; mix well. Add cheese, shallot, salt and pepper; blend well. Add spinach; mix well.

② Unroll dough; place on ungreased cookie sheet. Starting at center, press out dough with hands to 14×9-inch rectangle. In small bowl, combine remaining egg and water; mix well. Brush egg mixture lightly over dough; reserve remaining for top of braid.

③ Spread filling lengthwise in 4-inch-wide strip down center of dough to within ¼ inch of each end. With sharp knife, make cuts 1 inch apart on long sides of rectangle, just to edge of filling. Fold strips of dough alternately over filling to create braid (see diagram). Fold ends of braid under to seal. Brush top with reserved egg mixture.

④ Bake at 375° F. for 20 to 25 minutes or until golden brown. Cool 5 minutes. Serve warm.

Yield: 12 servings

NUTRITION INFORMATION:
SERVING SIZE: ¹⁄₁₂ OF RECIPE
CALORIES 130 (38% FROM FAT) • FAT 6 G
(SAT. 2 G) • CHOLESTEROL 50 MG
SODIUM 340 MG • CARBOHYDRATE 12 G
FIBER 1 G • PROTEIN 6 G

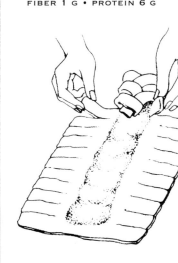

Vietnamese-Style Pork and Vegetable Salad

PREP TIME: 30 MINUTES

1 (6-OZ.) PKG. UNCOOKED RICE STICKS
   (RICE NOODLES), BROKEN
   IN HALF

1 TABLESPOON SESAME OIL

¾ LB. BONELESS PORK LOIN CHOPS,
   CUT LENGTHWISE INTO 2-INCH-
   WIDE STRIPS, THINLY SLICED

1 (1 LB. 5-OZ.) PKG. GREEN GIANT®
   CREATE A MEAL!® FROZEN
   TERIYAKI STIR FRY
   MEAL STARTER

2 CUPS SHREDDED LETTUCE

1 (8-OZ.) PKG. FRESH BEAN SPROUTS

(1) Cook rice sticks as directed on package. Drain; cover to keep warm.

(2) Meanwhile, heat oil in large skillet or wok over medium-high heat until hot. Add pork; cook and stir 2 to 3 minutes or until pork is no longer pink. Remove from skillet; cover to keep warm.

(3) In same skillet, combine frozen vegetables and frozen sauce from packet; mix well. Cover; cook 7 to 10 minutes or until vegetables are crisp-tender, stirring occasionally. Return pork to skillet; cook and stir until thoroughly heated.

(4) To serve, arrange cooked rice sticks on 6 individual plates; top each with lettuce, bean sprouts and pork mixture. If desired, serve with purchased teriyaki sauce.

Yield: 6 servings

NUTRITION INFORMATION:
SERVING SIZE: ⅙ OF RECIPE
CALORIES 280
(21% FROM FAT)
FAT 7 G (SAT. 2 G)
CHOLESTEROL 35 MG
SODIUM 470 MG
CARBOHYDRATE 36 G
FIBER 3 G
PROTEIN 18 G

Broccoli Rice Salad

PREP TIME: 35 MINUTES

1 (4.3-OZ.) PKG. HERB AND BUTTER
   FLAVOR RICE AND SAUCE MIX
1 (9-OZ.) PKG. GREEN GIANT®
   FROZEN CUT BROCCOLI
1 LARGE GREEN BELL PEPPER,
   CHOPPED
1 (15-OZ.) CAN GREEN GIANT®
   GARBANZO BEANS, DRAINED
2 TABLESPOONS CHOPPED FRESH
   CHIVES
½ TEASPOON GRATED LEMON PEEL
2 TABLESPOONS OIL
2 TABLESPOONS LEMON JUICE

1. Prepare rice and sauce mix as directed on package. Cool 15 minutes.

2. Meanwhile, cook broccoli as directed on package. Drain; cool 15 minutes.

3. In large bowl, combine cooked rice, cooked broccoli and all remaining ingredients; mix well. Serve immediately, or cover and refrigerate until serving time.

Yield: 4 (1½-cup) servings

NUTRITION INFORMATION: SERVING SIZE: 1½ CUPS
CALORIES 310 (32% FROM FAT) • FAT 11 G (SAT. 2 G) • CHOLESTEROL 5 MG
SODIUM 670 MG • CARBOHYDRATE 43 G • FIBER 7 G • PROTEIN 9 G

TIP

This green and white salad makes a nice accompaniment for roasted chicken or grilled steak. Round out the meal with tomato slices and scoops of sorbet with fresh fruit.

Hurry-Curry Corn Salad

BAKE-OFF® RECIPE
PREP TIME: 20 MINUTES

SALAD

- ⅓ CUP SLICED GREEN ONIONS
- ⅓ CUP CHOPPED CELERY
- 1 MEDIUM TOMATO, DICED
- 1 MEDIUM AVOCADO, PEELED, DICED
- 2 (11-OZ.) CANS GREEN GIANT® NIBLETS® EXTRA SWEET WHOLE KERNEL SWEET CORN, DRAINED

DRESSING

- ⅓ CUP SEASONED RICE VINEGAR
- ¼ CUP OIL
- 2 TO 3 TEASPOONS CURRY POWDER
- ½ TEASPOON SEASONED SALT

① In medium bowl, combine all salad ingredients; stir gently.

② In small bowl, combine all dressing ingredients; blend well. Pour dressing over salad; mix gently. Serve immediately, or cover and refrigerate until serving time.

Yield: 8 (½-cup) servings

NUTRITION INFORMATION: SERVING SIZE: ½ CUP
CALORIES 170 (59% FROM FAT) • FAT 11 G (SAT. 2 G) • CHOLESTEROL 0 MG
SODIUM 310 MG • CARBOHYDRATE 14 G • FIBER 4 G • PROTEIN 3 G

MAKING MEALS EASY

Texas Two-Step Slaw

BAKE-OFF® RECIPE

PREP TIME: 15 MINUTES

SALAD

4	CUPS SHREDDED GREEN CABBAGE
1	CUP SHREDDED RED CABBAGE
¼	CUP CHOPPED RED ONION
2	JALAPENO CHILES, SEEDED, FINELY CHOPPED*
2	TABLESPOONS CHOPPED FRESH CILANTRO
1	CUP SHREDDED CHEDDAR CHEESE
1	(11-OZ.) CAN GREEN GIANT® MEXICORN® WHOLE KERNEL CORN, RED AND GREEN PEPPERS, DRAINED

DRESSING

¾	CUP PURCHASED RANCH SALAD DRESSING
1	TABLESPOON LIME JUICE
1	TEASPOON CUMIN

1. In large bowl, combine all salad ingredients.

2. In small bowl, combine all dressing ingredients; blend well. Pour over salad; toss to coat. Serve immediately, or cover and refrigerate until serving time.

Yield: 8 (1-cup) servings

TIP: * WHEN HANDLING FRESH JALAPENO CHILES, WEAR PLASTIC OR RUBBER GLOVES TO PROTECT HANDS. DO NOT TOUCH FACE OR EYES.

NUTRITION INFORMATION: SERVING SIZE: 1 CUP
CALORIES 240 (71% FROM FAT) • FAT 19 G (SAT. 5 G) • CHOLESTEROL 20 MG
SODIUM 410 MG • CARBOHYDRATE 12 G • FIBER 2 G • PROTEIN 5 G

White Corn Salad

BAKE-OFF® RECIPE

PREP TIME: 15 MINUTES

2	TABLESPOONS OLIVE OIL
2	TABLESPOONS RICE VINEGAR
1	TEASPOON BROWN SUGAR
¼	TEASPOON SALT
⅛	TEASPOON PEPPER
2	(11-OZ.) CANS GREEN GIANT® WHITE SHOEPEG CORN, DRAINED
1	LARGE TOMATO, CHOPPED
3	TO 4 GREEN ONIONS, CHOPPED
½	GREEN BELL PEPPER, CHOPPED

1. In large bowl, combine oil, vinegar, brown sugar, salt and pepper; mix well.

2. Add corn, tomato, onions and bell pepper; toss to combine. Serve immediately, or cover and refrigerate until serving time.

Yield: 8 (½-cup) servings

NUTRITION INFORMATION: SERVING SIZE: ½ CUP
CALORIES 120 (29% FROM FAT) • FAT 4 G (SAT. 1 G) • CHOLESTEROL 0 MG
SODIUM 300 MG • CARBOHYDRATE 19 G • FIBER 2 G • PROTEIN 2 G

Top: Texas Two-Step Slaw
Bottom: White Corn Salad

Thai Noodle Salad

PREP TIME: 30 MINUTES

6   OZ. UNCOOKED LINGUINE
1   (9-OZ.) PKG. GREEN GIANT®
      FROZEN SUGAR SNAP PEAS
¼   CUP SOY SAUCE
¼   CUP VEGETABLE OR CHICKEN BROTH
2   TEASPOONS GRATED GINGERROOT
1   TABLESPOON PEANUT BUTTER
1   MEDIUM RED BELL PEPPER,
      CHOPPED (1 CUP)
¼   CUP CHOPPED FRESH CILANTRO
3   TABLESPOONS DRY-ROASTED
      PEANUTS

1. Cook linguine to desired doneness as directed on package. Drain; rinse with cold water to cool.

2. Meanwhile, cook sugar snap peas as directed on package. Drain; rinse with cold water to cool.

3. In large bowl, combine soy sauce, broth, gingerroot and peanut butter; mix until smooth. Stir in cooked linguine, cooked sugar snap peas and bell pepper; toss to coat. Sprinkle with cilantro and peanuts.

Yield: 3 (1²/₃-cup) servings

NUTRITION INFORMATION: SERVING SIZE: 1²/₃ CUPS
CALORIES 370 (19% FROM FAT) • FAT 8 G (SAT. 1 G) • CHOLESTEROL 0 MG
SODIUM 1660 MG • CARBOHYDRATE 59 G • FIBER 6 G • PROTEIN 15 G

Seven-Layer Chinese Chicken Salad

BAKE-OFF® RECIPE

PREP TIME: 15 MINUTES

SALAD

5 CUPS SHREDDED ROMAINE LETTUCE

1 (3-OZ.) PKG. ORIENTAL-FLAVOR RAMEN NOODLE SOUP MIX

2 CUPS DICED COOKED CHICKEN

1 (11-OZ.) CAN GREEN GIANT® WHITE SHOEPEG CORN, DRAINED

1 LARGE TOMATO, DICED

2 GREEN ONIONS, DICED

½ CUP COARSLEY CHOPPED UNSALTED DRY-ROASTED PEANUTS

DRESSING

2 TABLESPOONS SUGAR

1 TEASPOON SALT

¾ TEASPOON GRATED GINGERROOT

½ TEASPOON PEPPER

¼ CUP OIL

3 TABLESPOONS VINEGAR

1. Arrange romaine in bottom of large (3-quart) clear glass serving bowl. Discard seasoning packet from soup mix; coarsely crush noodles. Layer noodles and all remaining salad ingredients, in order listed, over romaine.

2. In small jar with tight-fitting lid, combine all dressing ingredients; shake until well blended. Pour over salad. Serve immediately.

Yield: 5 (2-cup) servings

NUTRITION INFORMATION: SERVING SIZE: 2 CUPS
CALORIES 460 (50% FROM FAT) • FAT 25 G (SAT. 5 G) • CHOLESTEROL 50 MG
SODIUM 1070 MG • CARBOHYDRATE 34 G • FIBER 4 G • PROTEIN 24 G

Chili, Soups & Stews

Familiar, hot, hearty, homey: These traditional meals-in-a-bowl soothe the soul at any time of the year.

What's more, several of these recipes yield slow-simmered goodness in 30 minutes or less.

Italian Pasta and Veggie Soup
(page 22)

Italian Pasta and Veggie Soup

PICTURED ON PAGES 20–21
PREP TIME: 15 MINUTES

1 (1 LB. 4.3-OZ.) PKG. GREEN GIANT® CREATE A MEAL!® FROZEN GARLIC HERB CHICKEN MEAL STARTER

1 (15-OZ.) CAN CANNELLINI BEANS

1 (14½-OZ.) CAN READY-TO-SERVE BEEF BROTH

¼ CUP WATER

½ CUP CHOPPED FRESH SPINACH, ROMAINE LETTUCE OR ENDIVE, IF DESIRED

SHREDDED FRESH PARMESAN CHEESE, IF DESIRED

① In Dutch oven or large saucepan, combine pasta and vegetables, sauce from packet, beans, broth and water. Cook over medium-high heat until sauce melts and mixture boils, stirring occasionally.

② Reduce heat; simmer 3 to 5 minutes or until pasta and vegetables are tender.

③ Stir in spinach; cook 1 minute. Sprinkle each serving with cheese.

Yield: 4 (1¼-cup) servings

NUTRITION INFORMATION: SERVING SIZE: 1¼ CUPS
CALORIES 250 (24% FROM FAT) • FAT 7 G (SAT. 4 G) • CHOLESTEROL 15 MG
SODIUM 1110 MG • CARBOHYDRATE 34 G • FIBER 6 G • PROTEIN 12 G

TIP

If you can't find Cannellini beans, Great Northern, navy or even red kidney beans all work well in this minestrone-style soup, too.

Confetti Wild Rice Soup

PREP TIME: 20 MINUTES (READY IN 8 HOURS 20 MINUTES)

⅔ CUP UNCOOKED WILD RICE, RINSED, DRAINED

½ CUP CHOPPED ONION

3 (14½-OZ.) CANS READY-TO-SERVE CHICKEN BROTH

2 MEDIUM CARROTS, THINLY SLICED (1 CUP)

½ TEASPOON DRIED MARJORAM LEAVES

⅛ TEASPOON PEPPER

2 BONELESS SKINLESS CHICKEN BREAST HALVES, CUT INTO ½-INCH PIECES

1½ CUPS GREEN GIANT® NIBLETS® FROZEN CORN, THAWED, DRAINED*

1 CUP GREEN GIANT® FROZEN BROCCOLI CUTS, THAWED, DRAINED*

① In 3½- to 4-quart slow cooker, combine all ingredients except thawed vegetables; mix well.

② Cover; cook on low setting for at least 8 hours.

③ Before serving, stir in thawed vegetables. Increase heat to high setting; cover and cook an additional 5 minutes or until vegetables are crisp-tender.

Yield: 6 servings

TIP: * TO QUICKLY THAW CORN AND BROCCOLI, PLACE IN COLANDER OR STRAINER; RINSE WITH WARM WATER UNTIL THAWED. DRAIN WELL.

NUTRITION INFORMATION: SERVING SIZE: ⅙ OF RECIPE
CALORIES 200 (13% FROM FAT) • FAT 3 G (SAT. 1 G) • CHOLESTEROL 25 MG
SODIUM 690 MG • CARBOHYDRATE 25 G • FIBER 3 G • PROTEIN 17 G

Quick Creamy Corn Soup

PREP TIME: 20 MINUTES

1 (15-OZ.) CAN GREEN GIANT® CREAM
   STYLE SWEET CORN
1 (11-OZ.) CAN GREEN GIANT®
   MEXICORN® WHOLE KERNEL
   CORN, RED AND GREEN PEPPERS,
   UNDRAINED
2 CUPS WATER
½ TEASPOON DRIED BASIL LEAVES
⅛ TEASPOON GARLIC POWDER
1 (8-OZ.) CONTAINER NONFAT OR
   LIGHT SOUR CREAM

1. In medium saucepan, combine all ingredients except sour cream. Bring to a boil. Reduce heat to medium; simmer 5 minutes to blend flavors.

2. Stir in sour cream; cook until thoroughly heated.

Yield: 4 (1⅓-cup) servings

NUTRITION INFORMATION: SERVING SIZE: 1⅓ CUPS
CALORIES 190 (5% FROM FAT) • FAT 1 G (SAT. 0 G) • CHOLESTEROL 0 MG
SODIUM 900 MG • CARBOHYDRATE 39 G • FIBER 3 G • PROTEIN 7 G

Southwestern Green Chile Soup

SALSA

- 2 (4.5-OZ.) CANS CHOPPED GREEN CHILES
- ¼ CUP PACKED FRESH CILANTRO LEAVES
- 1 TABLESPOON MINCED GARLIC IN WATER (FROM 4.5-OZ. JAR) OR 2 LARGE GARLIC CLOVES, MINCED
- 1 TEASPOON CUMIN
- DASH SALT

SOUP

- ¾ LB. FULLY COOKED SMOKED OR SPICY TURKEY SAUSAGE
- 2 TEASPOONS OLIVE OR VEGETABLE OIL
- ¼ CUP CHOPPED GREEN ONIONS
- 2 (14½-OZ.) CANS READY-TO-SERVE CHICKEN BROTH
- 2 (11-OZ.) CANS GREEN GIANT® WHITE SHOEPEG CORN, UNDRAINED
- 1 CUP GREEN GIANT SELECT® LESUEUR® FROZEN BABY SWEET PEAS
- 3 CUPS FINELY SHREDDED CABBAGE OR COLESLAW BLEND
- 3 OZ. (¾ CUP) SHREDDED MONTEREY JACK CHEESE
- 1 LARGE LIME, CUT INTO 6 WEDGES
- FRESH CILANTRO, IF DESIRED

① In blender container, combine all salsa ingredients except salt; blend until well combined. Add salt to taste. Set aside.

② Cut turkey sausage in half lengthwise; cut crosswise into ¼-inch-thick pieces. Heat oil in Dutch oven or large saucepan over medium-high heat until hot. Add sausage and onions; cook and stir 4 to 6 minutes or until sausage is lightly browned.

③ Add broth, corn and peas; mix well. Cover; bring to a boil. Uncover; reduce heat to low. Reserve ¼ cup of the salsa; stir remaining salsa into soup. Simmer 1 minute or until thoroughly heated.

④ To serve, place ½ cup cabbage in each individual serving bowl. Ladle about 1⅓ cups soup over cabbage. Top with cheese and reserved salsa. Serve with lime wedges to squeeze juice over soup. Garnish with cilantro.

Yield: 6 servings

NUTRITION INFORMATION:
SERVING SIZE: ⅙ OF RECIPE
CALORIES 330 (36% FROM FAT)
FAT 13 G (SAT. 6 G)
CHOLESTEROL 45 MG
SODIUM 1840 MG
CARBOHYDRATE 33 G
FIBER 5 G • PROTEIN 20 G

Easy Broccoli-Cheese Soup

PREP TIME: 25 MINUTES

2 TABLESPOONS MARGARINE
   OR BUTTER
½ CUP SHREDDED CARROT
½ CUP CHOPPED ONION
2 TABLESPOONS FLOUR
1 (15-OZ.) JAR CHEESE AND SALSA DIP
1 (14½-OZ.) CAN READY-TO-SERVE
   CHICKEN BROTH
1 (9-OZ.) PKG. GREEN GIANT® FROZEN
   CUT BROCCOLI, THAWED, LARGER
   PIECES CUT IN HALF
1 CUP MILK

1. Melt margarine in large saucepan over medium heat. Add carrot and onion; cook until tender, stirring occasionally. Sprinkle flour over vegetables; stir to blend.

2. Add all remaining ingredients; blend well. Cook over medium heat until thoroughly heated, stirring constantly.

Yield: 4 (1½-cup) servings

NUTRITION INFORMATION: SERVING SIZE: 1½ CUPS
CALORIES 300 (57% FROM FAT) • FAT 19 G (SAT. 5 G) • CHOLESTEROL 15 MG
SODIUM 1630 MG • CARBOHYDRATE 22 G • FIBER 3 G • PROTEIN 9 G

TIP

Serve this soup with warm flour tortillas and romaine lettuce drizzled with vinaigrette dressing.

Broccoli and Mushroom Soup

BAKE-OFF® RECIPE

PREP TIME: 30 MINUTES

2 TABLESPOONS OLIVE OIL OR
    VEGETABLE OIL

½ CUP CHOPPED ONION

1 GARLIC CLOVE, MINCED

1 (4-OZ.) CAN GREEN GIANT®
    MUSHROOM PIECES AND STEMS,
    DRAINED

4 CUPS CHICKEN OR VEGETABLE BROTH

1 (1-LB.) PKG. GREEN GIANT® FROZEN
    BROCCOLI CUTS

½ TEASPOON DRIED MARJORAM LEAVES

½ TEASPOON DRIED ROSEMARY LEAVES

3 OZ. LIGHT CREAM CHEESE,
    CUT INTO CUBES

½ CUP MASHED POTATO FLAKES

1. Heat oil in large saucepan or Dutch oven over medium heat until hot. Add onion, garlic and mushrooms; cook and stir 2 to 3 minutes or until onion is crisp-tender. With slotted spoon, remove vegetables; set aside.

2. In same saucepan, bring broth to a boil. Add broccoli, marjoram and rosemary; cook 5 to 7 minutes or until broccoli is tender. Reserve ½ cup broccoli florets (larger pieces can be cut smaller); set aside. To remaining broccoli mixture, add cream cheese and potato flakes.

3. In blender container or food processor bowl with metal blade, blend broccoli mixture until almost smooth. (If necessary, broccoli mixture can be processed in batches.)

4. In same saucepan, combine pureed broccoli mixture, reserved broccoli florets and reserved vegetables; cook until cheese is melted and mixture is thoroughly heated, stirring occasionally. If desired, garnish with lemon slices and fresh rosemary.

Yield: 6 (1-cup) servings

NUTRITION INFORMATION:
SERVING SIZE: 1 CUP
CALORIES 160 (50% FROM FAT)
FAT 9 G (SAT. 3 G) • CHOLESTEROL 10 MG
SODIUM 670 MG • CARBOHYDRATE 12 G
FIBER 3 G • PROTEIN 8 G

Lite Cheese Vegetable Chowder

PREP TIME: 30 MINUTES (READY IN 50 MINUTES)

2	TABLESPOONS MARGARINE OR BUTTER
2	CUPS CHOPPED CABBAGE
1	CUP SLICED ONIONS
1	CUP CHOPPED CELERY
1	CUP THINLY SLICED CARROTS
1	(15-OZ.) CAN GREEN GIANT® CREAM STYLE SWEET CORN
1	(8.5-OZ.) CAN GREEN GIANT® SWEET PEAS, DRAINED
2½	CUPS MILK
½	TEASPOON DRIED THYME LEAVES
¼	TEASPOON PEPPER
10	OZ. (2 CUPS) CUBED LIGHT PASTEURIZED PROCESS CHEESE PRODUCT

1. Melt margarine in Dutch oven or large saucepan over medium-high heat. Add cabbage, onions, celery and carrots; cook 8 to 10 minutes or until crisp-tender, stirring frequently.

2. Add corn, peas, milk, thyme and pepper. Reduce heat to medium; cook 15 to 20 minutes or until corn and peas are crisp-tender, stirring occasionally.

3. Add cheese; stir until melted. Heat gently, stirring frequently. DO NOT BOIL. If desired, add salt to taste.

Yield: 7 (1-cup) servings

NUTRITION INFORMATION: SERVING SIZE: 1 CUP
CALORIES 260 (38% FROM FAT) • FAT 11 G (SAT. 6 G) • CHOLESTEROL 25 MG
SODIUM 1000 MG • CARBOHYDRATE 27 G • FIBER 4 G • PROTEIN 13 G

TIP

Dress up this soup with a garnish of: chopped fresh herbs, sliced green onion, diced tomatoes, herbed croutons or paper-thin slices of fresh lemon.

Slow-Cooked Bean Cassoulet

PREP TIME: 15 MINUTES (READY IN 8 HOURS 15 MINUTES)

1   (16-OZ.) CAN VEGETARIAN BAKED
    BEANS, UNDRAINED
1   (15.5-OZ.) CAN GREEN GIANT®
    BUTTER BEANS, DRAINED, RINSED
1   (15.5 OR 15-OZ.) CAN GREEN
    GIANT® RED KIDNEY BEANS,
    DRAINED, RINSED
1   (14.5-OZ.) CAN STEWED TOMATOES
    WITH ITALIAN SEASONING,
    UNDRAINED, CUT UP
1   (9-OZ.) PKG. GREEN GIANT® FROZEN
    BABY LIMA BEANS
1   CUP THINLY SLICED CARROTS
1   CUP CHOPPED ONIONS
½   TEASPOON GARLIC SALT
⅛   TEASPOON FENNEL SEED, CRUSHED
⅛   TEASPOON GROUND RED PEPPER
    (CAYENNE)

① In 3½- to 4-quart slow cooker, combine all ingredients; mix well.

② Cover; cook on low setting for at least 8 hours or until vegetables are tender.

Yield: 6 (1¼-cup) servings

NUTRITION INFORMATION: SERVING SIZE: 1¼ CUPS
CALORIES 260 (4% FROM FAT) • FAT 1 G (SAT. 0 G) • CHOLESTEROL 0 MG
SODIUM 900 MG • CARBOHYDRATE 50 G • FIBER 13 G • PROTEIN 13 G

Spicy Black Bean Chili

PREP TIME: 25 MINUTES

1 CUP CHOPPED ONIONS

1 (15-OZ.) CAN SOUTHWESTERN-STYLE
BLACK BEANS WITH CUMIN AND
CHILI SPICES, UNDRAINED

1 (14.5-OZ.) CAN DICED TOMATOES
WITH CHILI OR SALSA
SEASONINGS, UNDRAINED

1 (11-OZ.) CAN GREEN GIANT®
MEXICORN® WHOLE KERNEL
CORN, RED AND GREEN PEPPERS

4 OZ. (1 CUP) SHREDDED CHEDDAR
CHEESE

1. Spray large nonstick skillet with nonstick cooking spray. Heat over medium-high heat until hot. Add onions; cook and stir until tender.

2. Stir in beans, tomatoes and corn. Bring to a boil. Reduce heat to low; simmer 5 to 8 minutes or until thoroughly heated.

3. Sprinkle with cheese; cover and cook an additional 1 to 2 minutes or until cheese is melted. If desired, serve with avocado dip, sour cream and fresh cilantro.

Yield: 4 (1-cup) servings

NUTRITION INFORMATION: SERVING SIZE: 1 CUP
CALORIES 320 (31% FROM FAT) • FAT 11 G (SAT. 6 G) • CHOLESTEROL 30 MG
SODIUM 1270 MG • CARBOHYDRATE 39 G • FIBER 10 G • PROTEIN 16 G

MAKING MEALS EASY

White Chili with Salsa Verde

BAKE-OFF® RECIPE

PREP TIME: 45 MINUTES (READY IN 1 HOUR 15 MINUTES)

SALSA VERDE*

2	CUPS COARSELY CHOPPED FRESH TOMATILLOS OR 2 (11-OZ.) CANS TOMATILLOS, CHOPPED, WELL DRAINED**
½	CUP CHOPPED ONION
½	CUP CHOPPED FRESH CILANTRO
1	PICKLED JALAPENO CHILE, CHOPPED
1	GARLIC CLOVE, MINCED
½	TEASPOON LEMON-PEPPER SEASONING
½	TEASPOON DRIED OREGANO LEAVES
½	TEASPOON ADOBO SEASONING OR GARLIC POWDER***
2	TO 3 TABLESPOONS LIME JUICE

CHILI

2½	CUPS WATER
1	TEASPOON LEMON-PEPPER SEASONING
1	TEASPOON CUMIN SEED
4	CHICKEN BREAST HALVES (ABOUT 1½ LB.), SKIN REMOVED
1	GARLIC CLOVE, MINCED
1	CUP CHOPPED ONIONS
2	(9-OZ.) PKG. GREEN GIANT® FROZEN SHOEPEG WHITE CORN, THAWED
2	(4.5-OZ.) CANS CHOPPED GREEN CHILES, UNDRAINED
1	TEASPOON CUMIN
2	TO 3 TABLESPOONS LIME JUICE
2	(15.5 OR 15-OZ.) CANS GREEN GIANT® GREAT NORTHERN BEANS, UNDRAINED
⅔	CUP CRUSHED TORTILLA CHIPS
2	OZ. (½ CUP) SHREDDED REDUCED-FAT MONTEREY JACK CHEESE

1. In medium bowl, combine all salsa ingredients; mix well. Refrigerate 30 minutes to blend flavors.

2. Meanwhile, in large saucepan, combine water, 1 teaspoon lemon-pepper seasoning and cumin seed. Bring to a boil. Add chicken. Reduce heat to low; cover and simmer 20 to 28 minutes or until chicken is fork-tender and juices run clear. Remove chicken from bones; cut into 1-inch pieces. Return chicken to saucepan.

3. Spray medium skillet with nonstick cooking spray. Heat over medium heat until hot. Add garlic; cook and stir 1 minute. Remove from skillet; add to chicken mixture.

4. Add 1 cup onions to skillet; cook and stir until tender. Add cooked onions, corn, chiles, cumin and 2 to 3 tablespoons lime juice to chicken mixture. Bring to a boil. Add beans; cook until thoroughly heated.

5. To serve, place about 1 tablespoon each of tortilla chips and cheese in each of 8 individual soup bowls; ladle soup over cheese. Serve with salsa.

Yield: 8 (1¼-cup) servings

TIPS: * IF DESIRED, SUBSTITUTE ONE 16-OZ. JAR SALSA VERDE (GREEN SALSA).
** IF FRESH OR CANNED TOMATILLOS ARE NOT AVAILABLE, 2 CUPS COARSELY CHOPPED GREEN TOMATOES CAN BE SUBSTITUTED.
*** ADOBO IS A SPECIALTY SEASONING AVAILABLE IN HISPANIC GROCERY STORES.

NUTRITION INFORMATION: SERVING SIZE: 1¼ CUPS
CALORIES 340 (18% FROM FAT) • FAT 7 G (SAT. 2 G) • CHOLESTEROL 55 MG
SODIUM 620 MG • CARBOHYDRATE 39 G • FIBER 9 G • PROTEIN 29 G

White Turkey Chili

2 TABLESPOONS OIL

1 CUP CHOPPED ONIONS

2 STALKS CELERY, THINLY SLICED

4 CUPS CHOPPED COOKED TURKEY

2 (15.5-OZ.) CANS GREEN GIANT®
  GREAT NORTHERN BEANS,
  DRAINED

2 (14½-OZ.) CANS READY-TO-SERVE
  CHICKEN BROTH

2 (11-OZ.) CANS GREEN GIANT®
  WHITE SHOEPEG CORN,
  UNDRAINED, OR 1 (1-LB.) PKG.
  GREEN GIANT SELECT® FROZEN
  WHITE SHOEPEG CORN

1 (4.5-OZ.) CAN CHOPPED GREEN
  CHILES

2 TEASPOONS CUMIN

¼ TEASPOON HOT PEPPER SAUCE,
  IF DESIRED

2 OZ. (½ CUP) SHREDDED MONTEREY
  JACK CHEESE

1 TABLESPOON CHOPPED FRESH
  PARSLEY

1. Heat oil in large saucepan over medium heat until hot. Add onions and celery; cook and stir 2 to 3 minutes or until vegetables are tender.

2. Stir in all remaining ingredients except cheese and parsley; blend well. Cover; cook 15 to 20 minutes or until thoroughly heated, stirring occasionally.

3. To serve, ladle chili into bowls. Sprinkle with cheese and parsley.

Yield: 12 (1-cup) servings

NUTRITION INFORMATION: SERVING SIZE: 1 CUP
CALORIES 240 (25% FROM FAT) • FAT 7 G (SAT. 2 G) • CHOLESTEROL 40 MG
SODIUM 580 MG • CARBOHYDRATE 23 G • FIBER 4 G • PROTEIN 21 G

Zesty Black and White Bean Chili

PREP TIME: 35 MINUTES

1   CUP CHOPPED ONIONS
1   GARLIC CLOVE, MINCED
¼   CUP FLOUR
1   TO 2 TEASPOONS CHILI POWDER
½   TEASPOON CUMIN
1½ CUPS MILK
2   (9-OZ.) PKG. GREEN GIANT® FROZEN
    SHOEPEG WHITE CORN
1   (15.5-OZ.) CAN GREEN GIANT®
    GREAT NORTHERN BEANS,
    DRAINED, RINSED
1   (15-OZ.) CAN GREEN GIANT® BLACK
    BEANS, DRAINED, RINSED
1   (14½-OZ.) CAN READY-TO-SERVE
    CHICKEN BROTH
1   (4.5-OZ.) CAN CHOPPED GREEN
    CHILES, UNDRAINED
2   TABLESPOONS CHOPPED FRESH
    CILANTRO
2   TABLESPOONS FINELY CHOPPED
    RED BELL PEPPER

1. Spray Dutch oven or large saucepan with nonstick cooking spray. Heat over medium-high heat until hot. Add onions and garlic; cook until onions are tender.

2. Stir in flour, chili powder and cumin. Gradually stir in milk. Add all remaining ingredients except cilantro and bell pepper; stir to combine.

3. Bring to a boil, stirring constantly. Reduce heat to low; simmer 15 minutes or until thickened, stirring occasionally. Stir in cilantro. If desired, add salt and pepper to taste.

4. To serve, spoon chili into serving bowls. Sprinkle with bell pepper.

Yield: 5 (1⅓-cup) servings

NUTRITION INFORMATION: SERVING SIZE: 1⅓ CUPS
CALORIES 320 • (11% FROM FAT) • FAT 4 G (SAT. 1 G) • CHOLESTEROL 5 MG
SODIUM 760 MG • CARBOHYDRATE 56 G • FIBER 12 G • PROTEIN 16 G

MAKING MEALS EASY

Skillet Dinners

Stovetop suppers, inspired by the best ingredients of international cuisines, come to the rescue when the evening calls

for a delicious quick-fix meal. Colorful, flavorful and sure to please young and old alike.

Teriyaki Chicken with Ramen Noodles
(page 38)

Teriyaki Chicken with Ramen Noodles

PICTURED ON PAGE 1 AND ON PAGES 36–37
PREP TIME: 20 MINUTES

1   TABLESPOON VEGETABLE OIL
2   BONELESS SKINLESS CHICKEN
       BREAST HALVES (ABOUT 8 OZ.),
       CUT INTO 1-INCH PIECES
1   (1 LB. 5-OZ.) PKG. GREEN GIANT®
       CREATE A MEAL!® FROZEN
       TERIYAKI STIR FRY MEAL
       STARTER
¾   CUP WATER
1   (3-OZ.) PKG. CHICKEN-FLAVOR
       RAMEN NOODLE SOUP MIX

1. Heat oil in large skillet or wok over medium-high heat until hot. Add chicken; cook and stir 3 to 4 minutes or until chicken is no longer pink.

2. Add frozen sauce from packet, water and ½ teaspoon seasoning mix. Discard remaining seasoning mix. Heat until sauce is thawed.

3. Break up noodles into pieces. Add noodles and frozen vegetables to skillet. Cover; cook 8 to 10 minutes until vegetables are crisp-tender, stirring frequently.

Yield: 4 (1¼-cup) servings

NUTRITION INFORMATION: SERVING SIZE: 1¼ CUPS
CALORIES 270 (30% FROM FAT) • FAT 9 G (SAT. 3 G) • CHOLESTEROL 35 MG
SODIUM 1000 MG • CARBOHYDRATE 27 G • FIBER 3 G • PROTEIN 19 G

Broccoli and Tortellini Alfredo

PREP TIME: 20 MINUTES

1   (14-OZ.) BAG GREEN GIANT
       SELECT® 100% BROCCOLI
       FLORETS
1   (19-OZ.) BAG FROZEN TORTELLINI
1   (10-OZ.) CONTAINER REFRIGERATED
       ALFREDO SAUCE OR 1 (1-LB.) JAR
       ALFREDO SAUCE
    SHREDDED FRESH PARMESAN CHEESE

1. Prepare broccoli and tortellini as directed on package. Drain; place in large serving bowl.

2. Meanwhile, heat Alfredo sauce in saucepan. Pour sauce over broccoli and tortellini; toss to coat. Sprinkle with Parmesan cheese.

Yield: 5 (1⅓-cup) servings

NUTRITION INFORMATION: SERVING SIZE: 1⅓ CUPS
CALORIES 470 (45% FROM FAT) • FAT 23 G (SAT. 12 G) • CHOLESTEROL 55 MG
SODIUM 610 MG • CARBOHYDRATE 49 G • FIBER 4 G • PROTEIN 16 G

Broccoli and Tortellini Alfredo

Coconut Curried Vegetables with Rice

1 CUP UNCOOKED REGULAR
    LONG-GRAIN WHITE RICE

2 CUPS WATER

2 TABLESPOONS FLOUR

1½ TEASPOONS CURRY POWDER

½ TEASPOON SALT

⅛ TEASPOON PEPPER

1 (14-OZ.) CAN LIGHT COCONUT MILK

1 TEASPOON LIME JUICE

1 (1-LB.) PKG. GREEN GIANT SELECT®
    FROZEN BROCCOLI, CARROTS
    AND CAULIFLOWER

1 CUP GREEN GIANT® FROZEN
    SWEET PEAS

1. Cook rice in 2 cups water as directed on package.

2. Meanwhile, in small bowl, combine flour, curry powder, salt, pepper and ¼ cup of the coconut milk; beat with wire whisk until smooth. Stir in remaining coconut milk and lime juice. Set aside.

3. In large saucepan, combine frozen vegetables, peas and ½ cup water. Bring to a boil. Reduce heat to low; cover and simmer 6 to 8 minutes or until vegetables are crisp-tender. Drain; set aside.

4. Pour coconut milk mixture into same saucepan. Bring to a boil, stirring constantly. Boil and stir 1 minute. Stir in vegetables. Cook over medium heat until thoroughly heated, stirring frequently. Serve over rice.

Yield: 4 servings

NUTRITION INFORMATION: SERVING SIZE: ¼ OF RECIPE
CALORIES 310 • (16% FROM FAT) • FAT 6 G (SAT. 5 G) • CHOLESTEROL 0 MG
SODIUM 420 MG • CARBOHYDRATE 55 G • FIBER 5 G • PROTEIN 8 G

Chili-Crusted Chicken and Rice Medley

PREP TIME: 35 MINUTES

RICE

2 (10-OZ.) PKG. GREEN GIANT® FROZEN RICE AND BROCCOLI IN CHEESE FLAVORED SAUCE

CHILI SPICE MIX

3 TEASPOONS CHILI POWDER

1 TEASPOON PAPRIKA

1 TEASPOON CUMIN

¼ TO ½ TEASPOON GARLIC SALT

¼ TEASPOON PEPPER

⅛ TEASPOON CINNAMON

CHICKEN

1 LB. BONELESS SKINLESS CHICKEN BREAST HALVES, CUT CROSSWISE INTO 3×1×¼-INCH STRIPS

2 TABLESPOONS OLIVE OR VEGETABLE OIL

1 (11-OZ.) CAN GREEN GIANT® NIBLETS® GOLDEN SWEET CORN, DRAINED

1 (15-OZ.) CAN GREEN GIANT® BLACK BEANS, DRAINED, RINSED

1. Cook rice as directed on package.

2. Meanwhile, in small bowl, combine all chili spice mix ingredients; mix well. Coat chicken strips with spice mix.

3. Heat oil in large skillet over medium heat until hot. Add chicken; cook and stir 8 to 10 minutes or until chicken is deep brown and no longer pink in center. Remove from skillet; cover to keep warm.

4. In same skillet, combine cooked rice, corn and black beans; mix well. Cover; cook over medium heat for 5 minutes, stirring occasionally. Add chicken; cook an additional 2 to 3 minutes or until thoroughly heated.

5. To serve, spoon rice mixture onto serving plate; arrange chicken strips on top. If desired, garnish with tomato wedges and fresh parsley.

Yield: 6 (1¼-cup) servings

NUTRITION INFORMATION: SERVING SIZE: 1¼ CUPS
CALORIES 340 • (24% FROM FAT) • FAT 9 G (SAT. 2 G)
CHOLESTEROL 45 MG
SODIUM 830 MG
CARBOHYDRATE 40 G
FIBER 5 G • PROTEIN 24 G

MAKING MEALS EASY

Apricot Beef Stir-Fry

PREP TIME: 35 MINUTES

1   (5.5-OZ.) CAN APRICOT NECTAR

3   TABLESPOONS PURCHASED LEMON
     STIR-FRY SAUCE

1   TABLESPOON CORNSTARCH

1   TABLESPOON VEGETABLE OIL

¾   LB. BONELESS BEEF TOP SIRLOIN
     STEAK, THINLY SLICED

1   TEASPOON CHILI OIL

1   SMALL ONION, CUT INTO THIN
     WEDGES

2   (7.5-OZ.) PKG. GREEN GIANT®
     FROZEN GREEN BEANS AND
     ALMONDS

1   (15-OZ.) CAN APRICOT HALVES,
     DRAINED, THINLY SLICED

1 In small bowl, combine ¼ cup of the apricot nectar, stir-fry sauce and cornstarch; blend until smooth. Set aside.

2 Heat vegetable oil in large skillet or wok over medium-high heat until hot. Add beef; cook and stir 2 to 3 minutes or until beef is browned. Remove from skillet; cover to keep warm.

3 In same skillet, heat chili oil over medium-high heat until hot. Add onion; cook and stir 2 minutes. Add remaining apricot nectar and green beans. Bring to a boil. Reduce heat to medium; cover and simmer 6 to 8 minutes or until vegetables are crisp-tender, stirring occasionally.

4 Increase heat to medium high. Stir cornstarch mixture until smooth; add to skillet. Cook and stir 2 to 3 minutes or until sauce is bubbly and thickened. Stir in apricots and beef; cook and stir until thoroughly heated. Sprinkle with almonds from packet.

Yield: 4 (1¼-cup) servings

NUTRITION INFORMATION: SERVING SIZE: 1¼ CUPS
CALORIES 280 (39% FROM FAT) • FAT 12 G (SAT. 2 G) • CHOLESTEROL 45 MG
SODIUM 560 MG • CARBOHYDRATE 25 G • FIBER 5 G • PROTEIN 19 G

TIP

serve the stir-fry atop a bed of rice for a heartier meal. Fragrant basmati and jasmine rices are especially good with the spicy-sweet beef.

Beef and Broccoli Pita Folds

PREP TIME: 20 MINUTES

½ CUP UNCOOKED INSTANT WHITE RICE

½ CUP WATER

1 (1 LB. 5-OZ.) PKG. GREEN GIANT®
   CREATE A MEAL!® FROZEN
   BROCCOLI STIR FRY
   MEAL STARTER

½ LB. BONELESS LEAN BEEF SIRLOIN
   STEAK

1 OZ. (¼ CUP) SHREDDED REDUCED-
   FAT CHEDDAR CHEESE

4 SOFT WHITE PITA FOLD BREADS

1. Cook rice in water as directed on package, omitting margarine and salt. Meanwhile, spray large nonstick skillet with nonstick cooking spray.

2. Prepare frozen broccoli stir fry meal starter as directed on package, using steak but omitting oil.

3. Remove skillet from heat. Add cooked rice and cheese; mix well. Cover; let stand 1 to 2 minutes or until cheese is slightly melted.

4. To serve, spoon beef-vegetable mixture into pita fold breads.

Yield: 4 sandwiches

NUTRITION INFORMATION: SERVING SIZE: 1 SANDWICH
CALORIES 370 (16% FROM FAT) • FAT 7 G (SAT. 2 G) • CHOLESTEROL 35 MG
SODIUM 1170 MG • CARBOHYDRATE 54 G • FIBER 5 G • PROTEIN 22 G

SKILLET DINNERS

Cheesy Fish and Vegetables

PREP TIME: 20 MINUTES

1 LB. COD OR HALIBUT FILLETS, CUT
    INTO SERVING-SIZED PIECES

¼ CUP DRY WHITE WINE OR
    CHICKEN BROTH

1 TEASPOON DRIED PARSLEY FLAKES

1 (10-OZ.) PKG. GREEN GIANT®
    FROZEN BROCCOLI, CAULIFLOWER
    AND CARROTS IN CHEESE
    FLAVORED SAUCE

1. Place cod fillets in large skillet; add wine and parsley. Cover; cook 5 to 10 minutes or until fish flakes easily with fork.

2. Meanwhile, cook vegetables as directed on package.

3. Remove fish from skillet; place on warm serving platter. Add hot vegetable mixture to hot cooking liquid in skillet; mix well. Spoon mixture over fish.

Yield: 4 servings

NUTRITION INFORMATION: SERVING SIZE: ¼ OF RECIPE
CALORIES 140 (14% FROM FAT) • FAT 2 G (SAT. 1 G) • CHOLESTEROL 50 MG
SODIUM 350 MG • CARBOHYDRATE 6 G • FIBER 1 G • PROTEIN 22 G

Easy Nacho Skillet Dinner

PREP TIME: 25 MINUTES

1 LB. GROUND BEEF

1 (15.5-OZ.) CAN GREEN GIANT®
   KIDNEY BEANS, DRAINED, RINSED

1 (15-OZ.) CAN TOMATO SAUCE

1 (11-OZ.) CAN GREEN GIANT®
   MEXICORN® WHOLE KERNEL
   CORN, RED AND GREEN PEPPERS,
   UNDRAINED

1 TEASPOON CHILI POWDER

2 CUPS SLIGHTLY BROKEN TORTILLA
   CHIPS

4 OZ. (1 CUP) SHREDDED CHEDDAR
   CHEESE

1 In large skillet over medium-high heat, brown ground beef until thoroughly cooked; drain.

2 Stir in beans, tomato sauce, corn and chili powder. Reduce heat to low; simmer 10 minutes, stirring occasionally.

3 Sprinkle tortilla chips evenly over beef mixture; top with cheese. Cover; simmer 2 minutes or until cheese is melted.

Yield: 6 servings

NUTRITION INFORMATION: SERVING SIZE: 1/6 OF RECIPE
CALORIES 440 (45% FROM FAT) • FAT 22 G (SAT. 9 G) • CHOLESTEROL 65 MG
SODIUM 1060 MG • CARBOHYDRATE 36 G • FIBER 6 G • PROTEIN 25 G

TIP

To reduce fat, substitute ground turkey for beef. It has 8 grams of fat per 3 ounces cooked, compared to about 15 grams for 80% lean ground beef.

Pasta Primavera with Chicken

PREP TIME: 25 MINUTES

8   OZ. UNCOOKED PENNE PASTA
2   (9-OZ.) PKG. GREEN GIANT® FROZEN
      VEGETABLES ALFREDO
1   LB. PRECUT CHICKEN STRIPS FOR
      STIR-FRYING
1   TABLESPOON OIL
½   CUP MILK
¼   CUP SHREDDED FRESH PARMESAN
      CHEESE

① Cook pasta as directed on package. Drain; cover to keep warm.

② Cook vegetables as directed on package.

③ Meanwhile, in large skillet, cook chicken in oil until no longer pink.

④ To chicken in skillet, add cooked pasta, cooked vegetables and milk; toss gently to mix. Sprinkle with cheese.

Yield: 4 (2½-cup) servings

NUTRITION INFORMATION: SERVING SIZE: ¼ OF RECIPE
CALORIES 570 (37% FROM FAT) • FAT 23 G (SAT. 7 G) • CHOLESTEROL 135 MG
SODIUM 850 MG • CARBOHYDRATE 59 G • FIBER 5 G • PROTEIN 32 G

TIP

This flavorful vegetable-studded pasta dish needs nothing more than a spinach-orange salad or sliced garlic bread to round out the menu.

Taco and Black Bean Skillet Dinner

PREP TIME: 30 MINUTES

1 (24-OZ.) JAR CHUNKY-STYLE SALSA
   OR PICANTE
1 (4.6-OZ.) PKG. (12 SHELLS) TACO
   SHELLS
4 OZ. (1 CUP) SHREDDED MONTEREY
   JACK CHEESE
4 OZ. (1 CUP) SHREDDED CHEDDAR
   CHEESE
1 (11-OZ.) CAN GREEN GIANT® WHITE
   SHOEPEG CORN, DRAINED
1 (4.5-OZ.) CAN CHOPPED GREEN
   CHILES
1 SMALL ONION, CHOPPED (¼ CUP)
1 (15-OZ.) CAN GREEN GIANT® BLACK
   BEANS, DRAINED
2 TEASPOONS CUMIN
1 TABLESPOON STEAK SAUCE

GARNISH
½ TO 1 CUP SOUR CREAM
   FRESH CILANTRO SPRIGS, IF
      DESIRED
   CHOPPED FRESH TOMATOES,
      IF DESIRED
   SLICED RIPE OLIVES, IF DESIRED
   CHOPPED JALAPENO CHILES,
      IF DESIRED
   GUACAMOLE, IF DESIRED

(1) Spray deep 10-inch skillet with nonstick cooking spray. Spread 1 cup of the salsa over bottom of sprayed skillet. Break each taco shell into 4 to 6 pieces. Arrange half of the broken shells over salsa. Spread 1 cup of the remaining salsa over shells. Sprinkle with ½ cup each of the Monterey Jack cheese and Cheddar cheese. Top with corn, green chiles and onion.

(2) In small bowl, combine beans, cumin and steak sauce; mix well. Spoon evenly over mixture in skillet. Top with remaining broken shells, Monterey Jack cheese, Cheddar cheese and salsa. Cover; cook over medium-low heat 15 to 20 minutes or until mixture is bubbly and cheese is melted.

(3) To serve, top with ½ cup of the sour cream; garnish with cilantro, tomatoes, olives, jalapeno chiles and guacamole. If desired, serve with remaining ½ cup sour cream.

Yield: 5 (1½-cup) servings

NUTRITION INFORMATION:
SERVING SIZE: 1½ CUPS
CALORIES 630
(51% FROM FAT)
FAT 36 G (SAT. 18 G)
CHOLESTEROL 65 MG
SODIUM 1740 MG
CARBOHYDRATE 56 G
FIBER 8 G
PROTEIN 21 G

Green Giant Rice Wraps

PREP TIME: 10 MINUTES

1 (10-OZ.) PKG. GREEN GIANT®
   FROZEN RICE AND BROCCOLI IN
   CHEESE FLAVORED SAUCE

½ CUP FROZEN DICED COOKED
   CHICKEN BREAST

4 MEDIUM FLOUR TORTILLAS

2 CUPS SHREDDED LETTUCE

2 OZ. (½ CUP) SHREDDED
   CHEDDAR CHEESE

4 TABLESPOONS SALSA

① Open rice pouch; combine rice mixture and chicken in large skillet. Cook over medium heat until thoroughly heated, stirring frequently.

② Meanwhile, heat tortillas as directed on package.

③ Place ½ cup lettuce on each tortilla; spoon about ⅓ cup chicken mixture on top of lettuce. Sprinkle with cheese and 1 tablespoon salsa. Fold up bottom; fold in sides to enclose filling and roll up.

Yield: 4 wraps

NUTRITION INFORMATION: SERVING SIZE: 1 WRAP
CALORIES 280 (29% FROM FAT) • FAT 9 G (SAT. 4 G) • CHOLESTEROL 30 MG
SODIUM 630 MG • CARBOHYDRATE 35 G • FIBER 2 G • PROTEIN 14 G

TIP

For a fun touch, wrap this tasty chicken filling in flavored tortillas. They add variety and color to this main dish.

Linguine Chicken Primavera

PREP TIME: 35 MINUTES

8 OZ. UNCOOKED LINGUINE

1 LB. BONELESS SKINLESS CHICKEN
   BREAST HALVES, CUT INTO
   1-INCH PIECES

1 (1-OZ.) PKG. RANCH SALAD
   DRESSING MIX

1 TABLESPOON MARGARINE OR BUTTER

1 GARLIC CLOVE, MINCED

1 (1-LB.) PKG. GREEN GIANT SELECT®
   FROZEN BROCCOLI, CARROTS
   AND CAULIFLOWER

1 CUP SKIM MILK

¼ CUP LIGHT CREAM CHEESE
   (FROM 8-OZ. TUB)

2 OZ. (½ CUP) SHREDDED FRESH
   PARMESAN CHEESE

① Cook linguine to desired doneness as directed on package. Drain; cover to keep warm.

② Meanwhile, in resealable food storage plastic bag, combine chicken and 2 tablespoons of the salad dressing mix; shake to coat.

③ Melt margarine in 12-inch nonstick skillet over medium-high heat. Add garlic; cook 1 minute. Add chicken; cook and stir 4 to 6 minutes or until chicken is lightly browned.

④ Add frozen vegetables; cover and cook 6 to 8 minutes or until chicken is no longer pink and vegetables are crisp-tender, stirring occasionally.

⑤ In small bowl, combine milk and remaining salad dressing mix; mix well. Reduce heat to medium; stir milk mixture and cream cheese into chicken mixture. Cook 1 to 2 minutes or until slightly thickened, stirring constantly. Add cooked linguine and Parmesan cheese; toss gently to mix.

Yield: 4 (2-cup) servings

NUTRITION INFORMATION:
SERVING SIZE: 2 CUPS
CALORIES 500 (24% FROM FAT) • FAT 13 G
(SAT. 5 G) • CHOLESTEROL 85 MG
SODIUM 470 MG • CARBOHYDRATE 53 G
FIBER 4 G • PROTEIN 42 G

Speedy Sweet and Sour Chicken

PREP TIME: 20 MINUTES

1½ CUPS UNCOOKED INSTANT WHITE RICE

1½ CUPS WATER

1 (10.5-OZ.) PKG. FROZEN BREADED
    PRECOOKED CHICKEN NUGGETS

2 TEASPOONS OIL

1 (1 LB. 5-OZ.) PKG. GREEN GIANT®
   CREATE A MEAL!® FROZEN SWEET
   & SOUR STIR FRY MEAL STARTER

1. Cook rice in water as directed on package.

2. Meanwhile, cook chicken in oil as directed on package until thoroughly heated. Remove from skillet.

3. Add frozen vegetables and pineapple and frozen sauce from packet to skillet. Cover; cook 7 to 10 minutes or until vegetables are crisp-tender, stirring frequently. Stir in cooked chicken. Serve over rice.

Yield: 3 servings

NUTRITION INFORMATION: SERVING SIZE: ⅓ OF RECIPE
CALORIES 520 (35% FROM FAT) • FAT 20 G (SAT. 4 G) • CHOLESTEROL 20 MG
SODIUM 1080 MG • CARBOHYDRATE 68 G • FIBER 7 G • PROTEIN 16 G

TIP

To intensify the flavor of this one-dish meal, cook the rice in chicken broth instead of water.

MAKING MEALS EASY

Springtime Orzo

BAKE-OFF® RECIPE

PREP TIME: 25 MINUTES

1   CUP UNCOOKED ORZO OR
      ROSAMARINA (RICE-SHAPED
      PASTA)
1   TABLESPOON BUTTER OR MARGARINE
½   CUP CHOPPED GREEN ONIONS
¼   CUP CHOPPED GREEN BELL PEPPER
6   OZ. CANADIAN BACON, DICED
1   (9-OZ.) PKG. GREEN GIANT® FROZEN
      SUGAR SNAP PEAS
½   TEASPOON LEMON-PEPPER
      SEASONING
¼   TO ½ TEASPOON SALT
½   CUP HALF-AND-HALF
2   TABLESPOONS SHREDDED FRESH
      PARMESAN CHEESE
2   TABLESPOONS CHOPPED FRESH
      PARSLEY

1. In Dutch oven or large saucepan, cook orzo in lightly salted boiling water for 6 to 8 minutes or just until tender. Drain; keep warm.

2. In same Dutch oven, melt butter over medium-high heat. Add onions, bell pepper and bacon; cook and stir 1 to 2 minutes or until onions are tender. Reduce heat to medium. Add sugar snap peas; cook 2 minutes.

3. Reduce heat to low. Stir in lemon-pepper seasoning, salt and half-and-half. Simmer 2 minutes or until warm. Stir in cheese, parsley and cooked orzo.

Yield: 3 (1⅓-cup) servings

NUTRITION INFORMATION: SERVING SIZE: 1⅓ CUPS
CALORIES 450 (29% FROM FAT) • FAT 14 G (SAT. 7 G) • CHOLESTEROL 55 MG
SODIUM 1440 MG • CARBOHYDRATE 56 G • FIBER 5 G • PROTEIN 24 G

TIP

For variety, substitute another small-size pasta such as tiny shells or ring macaroni for orzo; substitute red or yellow bell pepper for the green.

Twice-Cooked Noodles with Stir-Fried Vegetables

8 OZ. UNCOOKED FRESH CHINESE
   NOODLES OR ANGEL HAIR PASTA

1 TABLESPOON SOY SAUCE

1 TABLESPOON SESAME OIL

2 TABLESPOONS PEANUT OIL

1 (1 LB. 5-OZ.) PKG. GREEN GIANT®
   CREATE A MEAL!® FROZEN
   TERIYAKI OR GARLIC AND GINGER
   STIR FRY MEAL STARTER

1 CUP GREEN GIANT® FROZEN
   SWEET PEAS

¼ CUP SLIVERED ALMONDS

① Cook noodles as directed on package. Drain well. In large bowl, combine noodles, soy sauce and sesame oil; mix well.

② Heat 1 tablespoon of the peanut oil in large nonstick skillet or wok over medium-high heat until hot. Add noodle mixture, pressing to form thin pancake; cook 8 to 12 minutes or until bottom of noodle pancake is golden brown.

③ Slide pancake from skillet onto plate; invert pancake onto another plate, browned side up. Add remaining 1 tablespoon peanut oil to skillet. Slide noodle pancake into skillet, browned side up; cook 4 to 6 minutes or until bottom is browned. Slide onto serving plate; cover to keep warm.

④ In same skillet, add frozen sauce from packet. Stir in frozen vegetables and peas. Cover; cook 7 to 10 minutes or until vegetables are crisp-tender, stirring occasionally.

⑤ To serve, with sharp knife or kitchen scissors, cut hot noodle pancake into 4 wedges. Top pancake with vegetable mixture; sprinkle with almonds.

Yield: 4 servings

NUTRITION INFORMATION: SERVING SIZE: ¼ OF RECIPE
CALORIES 410 (37% FROM FAT) • FAT 17 G (SAT. 3 G) • CHOLESTEROL 60 MG
SODIUM 960 MG • CARBOHYDRATE 51 G • FIBER 7 G • PROTEIN 14 G

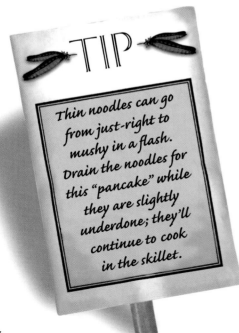

TIP

Thin noodles can go from just-right to mushy in a flash. Drain the noodles for this "pancake" while they are slightly underdone; they'll continue to cook in the skillet.

Ramen Vegetable Steak Stir-Fry

1	LB. BEEF TIP STEAKS (¼ INCH THICK), CUT CROSSWISE INTO 1-INCH-WIDE STRIPS
2	GARLIC CLOVES, MINCED
1	TABLESPOON SESAME OR VEGETABLE OIL
¼	TEASPOON GROUND RED PEPPER (CAYENNE)
1	(3-OZ.) PKG. ORIENTAL-FLAVOR RAMEN NOODLE SOUP MIX
2	CUPS WATER
1	(1-LB.) PKG. GREEN GIANT SELECT® FROZEN BROCCOLI, CARROTS AND WATER CHESTNUTS
1	TEASPOON SESAME OR VEGETABLE OIL
1	(4.5-OZ.) JAR GREEN GIANT® WHOLE MUSHROOMS, DRAINED
1	TABLESPOON SOY SAUCE

① In medium bowl, combine beef strips, garlic, 1 tablespoon sesame oil and ground red pepper; toss to coat. Set aside.

② Remove noodles from package; reserve seasoning packet. Bring water to a boil in large saucepan. Break block of noodles into 3 pieces; add to water with frozen vegetables. Return to a boil. Reduce heat; simmer uncovered 2 to 3 minutes or until vegetables are crisp-tender, stirring occasionally. Drain well. Return vegetable mixture to saucepan; stir in seasoning from packet. Cover; keep warm.

③ Rub 1 teaspoon sesame oil over large skillet or wok; heat over medium-high heat until hot. Add beef strips; cook and stir 1 to 2 minutes or until meat is no longer pink. Stir in vegetable mixture, mushrooms and soy sauce; cook until thoroughly heated.

Yield: 4 (1½-cup) servings

NUTRITION INFORMATION:
SERVING SIZE: 1 ½ CUPS
CALORIES 330 (39% FROM FAT)
FAT 14 G (SAT. 4 G)
CHOLESTEROL 60 MG
SODIUM 880 MG
CARBOHYDRATE 24 G
FIBER 4 G • PROTEIN 27 G

Skillet Teriyaki Chicken

PREP TIME: 25 MINUTES (READY IN 6 HOURS 25 MINUTES)

3 TO 3½ LB. CUT-UP OR QUARTERED
   FRYING CHICKEN, SKINNED
½ CUP TERIYAKI SAUCE
1 TABLESPOON OIL
1 (1-LB.) PKG. GREEN GIANT SELECT®
   FROZEN BROCCOLI, CARROTS
   AND WATER CHESTNUTS

(1) Place chicken pieces in shallow nonmetal dish or resealable food storage plastic bag. Pour teriyaki sauce over chicken. Cover dish or seal bag; refrigerate 6 to 8 hours to marinate, turning several times.

(2) Heat oil in large skillet over medium heat until hot. Remove chicken from marinade; reserve marinade for sauce. Add chicken to skillet; cook until browned on both sides.

(3) Add reserved marinade to skillet. Bring to a boil. Reduce heat to medium-low; cover and cook 25 to 30 minutes or until chicken is fork-tender and juices run clear.

(4) Meanwhile, cook frozen vegetables as directed on package.

(5) Remove chicken from skillet; cover to keep warm. Bring sauce to a boil; boil until slightly thickened. Serve chicken and sauce over vegetables.

Yield: 4 servings

NUTRITION INFORMATION: SERVING SIZE: ¼ OF RECIPE
CALORIES 330 (36% FROM FAT) • FAT 13 G (SAT. 3 G) • CHOLESTEROL 115 MG
SODIUM 1530 MG • CARBOHYDRATE 13 G • FIBER 2 G • PROTEIN 41 G

TIP

The chicken can be marinated the night before so you can prep this meal in 30 minutes or less.

The Giant's Macaroni and Cheese

1 (15 ¾-oz.) can low sodium chicken broth

4 oz. (1 cup) uncooked elbow macaroni

1 (10-oz.) pkg. Green Giant® Frozen Broccoli in Cheese Flavored Sauce

2 oz. (½ cup) shredded sharp Cheddar cheese

2 tablespoons grated Parmesan cheese

1 In medium saucepan, bring broth to a boil. Add macaroni; return to a boil. Cook 8 to 10 minutes or until macaroni is tender and a slight amount of broth remains. Do not drain.

2 Meanwhile, microwave broccoli as directed on package.

3 Add broccoli and Cheddar cheese to cooked macaroni; toss gently to mix. Sprinkle with Parmesan cheese. If desired, garnish with cherry tomatoes and fresh parsley.

Yield: 2 (1⅓-cup) servings

NUTRITION INFORMATION: Serving Size: 1⅓ Cups
CALORIES 310 (32% FROM FAT) • FAT 11 G (SAT. 6 G) • CHOLESTEROL 30 MG
SODIUM 730 MG • CARBOHYDRATE 37 G • FIBER 3 G • PROTEIN 15 G

TIP

Let the children choose the shape of pasta for this family-favorite recipe. Cavatelli, bow ties, wagon wheels or novelty-shaped pastas all work fine.

Spicy Chicken and Broccoli Stir-Fry

1   LB. BOK CHOY (ABOUT 7 STALKS)

2   TEASPOONS VEGETABLE OIL

1   TEASPOON CHILI OIL

4   BONELESS SKINLESS CHICKEN
      BREAST HALVES (ABOUT 1 LB.),
      CUT INTO 1-INCH PIECES

1   (1 LB. 5-OZ.) PKG. GREEN GIANT®
      CREATE A MEAL!® FROZEN
      BROCCOLI STIR FRY MEAL
      STARTER

½   CUP CHOW MEIN NOODLES

1. Separate bok choy leaves from stems. Cut leaves into 2-inch pieces; cut stems into ¼-inch slices. Set aside.

2. Heat vegetable and chili oils in large skillet or wok over medium-high heat until hot. Add chicken; cook and stir 5 to 7 minutes or until chicken is no longer pink.

3. Stir in frozen vegetables, frozen sauce from packet and sliced bok choy stems. Cover; cook 6 to 8 minutes or until vegetables are crisp-tender, stirring occasionally.

4. Add bok choy leaves; cook and stir 3 to 4 minutes or until leaves are slightly wilted. Sprinkle with chow mein noodles.

Yield: 4 (1¼-cup) servings

NUTRITION INFORMATION: SERVING SIZE: 1¼ CUPS
CALORIES 300 (33% FROM FAT) • FAT 11 G • (SAT. 2 G) • CHOLESTEROL 65 MG
SODIUM 980 MG • CARBOHYDRATE 18 G • FIBER 5 G • PROTEIN 31 G

Chicken and Vegetable Lo Mein

PREP TIME: 20 MINUTES

1   TABLESPOON SESAME OIL
3   BONELESS SKINLESS CHICKEN
      BREAST HALVES (ABOUT ¾ LB.),
      DICED
1   (1 LB. 5-OZ.) PKG. GREEN GIANT®
      CREATE A MEAL!® FROZEN
      LO MEIN STIR FRY MEAL
      STARTER
4   OZ. (1 CUP) FRESH SNOW PEA PODS
3   TABLESPOONS CHOPPED
      DRY-ROASTED PEANUTS

1. Heat oil in large skillet or wok over medium-high heat until hot. Add chicken; cook and stir 2 to 3 minutes or until no longer pink. Remove from skillet; cover to keep warm.

2. In same skillet, combine frozen vegetables and noodles, frozen sauce from packet and pea pods; mix well. Cover; cook 7 to 10 minutes or until vegetables are crisp-tender.

3. Return chicken to skillet; mix well. Cook and stir until thoroughly heated. Sprinkle with peanuts.

Yield: 4 (1¼-cup) servings

NUTRITION INFORMATION: SERVING SIZE: 1 ¼ CUPS
CALORIES 280 • (29% FROM FAT) • FAT 9 G (SAT. 2 G) • CHOLESTEROL 50 MG
SODIUM 780 MG • CARBOHYDRATE 24 G • FIBER 4 G • PROTEIN 25 G

Casseroles

From the classic elegance of creamy Chicken Divan to the down-home satisfaction of zesty Barbecue Chicken Cornmeal Bake, easily

prepared oven-baked suppers are enduring favorites of families everywhere.

Mexican Spinach Casserole
(page 66)

Mexican Spinach Casserole

PICTURED ON PAGES 64–65
PREP TIME: 20 MINUTES (READY IN 40 MINUTES)

1 (10-OZ.) PKG. GREEN GIANT® FROZEN CREAMED SPINACH

1 (7-OZ.) PKG. (3½ CUPS) UNCOOKED ELBOW MACARONI

1 (10-OZ.) CAN TOMATOES WITH CHILES, UNDRAINED

½ CUP SOUR CREAM

6 OZ. (1½ CUPS) SHREDDED CHEDDAR CHEESE

1. Heat oven to 350°F. Prepare spinach and cook macaroni as directed on packages.

2. In ungreased 12×8-inch (2-quart) baking dish, combine cooked spinach, cooked macaroni, tomatoes with chiles, sour cream and half of the cheese; mix well. Top with remaining cheese.

3. Bake at 350°F. for 20 minutes or until thoroughly heated and cheese is melted.

Yield: 6 servings

NUTRITION INFORMATION: SERVING SIZE: ⅙ OF RECIPE
CALORIES 320 (44% FROM FAT) • FAT 15 G (SAT. 9 G) • CHOLESTEROL 40 MG
SODIUM 520 MG • CARBOHYDRATE 33 G • FIBER 2 G • PROTEIN 14 G

TIP

Accompany this soothing, creamy casserole with crusty French bread, warmed in the oven, and a tossed green salad.

CASSEROLES

Baked Beef and Ravioli

PREP TIME: 20 MINUTES (READY IN 50 MINUTES)

1 (9-OZ.) PKG. REFRIGERATED CHEESE-FILLED RAVIOLI

1 LB. LEAN GROUND BEEF

1 (14-OZ.) JAR SPAGHETTI SAUCE

1 (9-OZ.) PKG. GREEN GIANT® FROZEN SPINACH, THAWED, SQUEEZED TO DRAIN

4 OZ. (1 CUP) SHREDDED MOZZARELLA CHEESE

1 Heat oven to 350°F. Cook ravioli to desired doneness as directed on package. Drain.

2 Meanwhile, in large skillet, brown ground beef until thoroughly cooked. Drain. Stir in spaghetti sauce and spinach.

3 Spoon and spread half of the beef mixture into ungreased 8-inch square (2-quart) baking dish. Arrange cooked ravioli over beef layer. Spoon and spread remaining beef mixture over ravioli. Cover with foil.

4 Bake at 350°F. for 20 minutes. Uncover; sprinkle with cheese. Bake uncovered for an additional 5 to 10 minutes or until casserole is bubbly and cheese is melted. If desired, garnish with yellow tomatoes and fresh parsley.

Yield: 4 servings

NUTRITION INFORMATION: SERVING SIZE: ¼ OF RECIPE
CALORIES 570 (46% FROM FAT) • FAT 29 G • (SAT. 13 G) • CHOLESTEROL 140 MG
SODIUM 1010 MG • CARBOHYDRATE 37 G • FIBER 4 G • PROTEIN 41 G

Spinach and Sausage Phyllo Bake

PREP TIME: 50 MINUTES (READY IN 1 HOUR 55 MINUTES)

1   LB. BULK PORK OR ITALIAN SAUSAGE
½   CUP THINLY SLICED ROASTED
        RED BELL PEPPERS
        (FROM 7.25-OZ. JAR)
1   (2¼-OZ.) CAN SLICED RIPE OLIVES,
        DRAINED
4   OZ. (1 CUP) SHREDDED MOZZARELLA
        CHEESE
5   EGGS, BEATEN
4   OZ. (1 CUP) SHREDDED CHEDDAR
        CHEESE
1   CUP RICOTTA CHEESE
1   (9-OZ.) PKG. GREEN GIANT® FROZEN
        SPINACH, THAWED, SQUEEZED TO
        DRAIN
16 (17×12-INCH) SHEETS FROZEN
        PHYLLO (FILO) PASTRY, THAWED
½   CUP BUTTER, MELTED

(1) Heat oven to 350°F. In large skillet, brown sausage over medium heat. Drain. Cool slightly. Stir in roasted peppers, olives, mozzarella cheese and eggs; mix well.

(2) In medium bowl, combine Cheddar cheese, ricotta cheese and spinach; mix well.

(3) Unroll phyllo pastry; cover with plastic wrap or towel. Place 1 sheet of phyllo in ungreased 13×9-inch (3-quart) baking dish, folding to fit. Brush lightly with melted butter. Continue layering and brushing with butter using 3 additional sheets of phyllo.

(4) Spoon half of sausage mixture over phyllo in baking dish. Layer and brush with butter 4 more phyllo sheets. Top with spinach mixture. Layer and brush with butter 4 more phyllo sheets. Top with remaining sausage mixture. Layer and brush with butter 4 more phyllo sheets. Score top of phyllo in diamond shapes.

(5) Bake at 350°F. for 50 to 60 minutes or until puffed and golden brown. Let stand 5 minutes before serving.

Yield: 8 servings

NUTRITION INFORMATION: SERVING SIZE: ⅛ OF RECIPE
CALORIES 550 (62% FROM FAT) • FAT 38 G (SAT. 19 G) • CHOLESTEROL 230 MG
SODIUM 1070 MG • CARBOHYDRATE 25 G • FIBER 2 G • PROTEIN 27 G

Creamy Roasted Veggies and Chicken Dijon

PREP TIME: 10 MINUTES (READY IN 45 MINUTES)

1   LB. PRECUT CHICKEN STRIPS FOR
    STIR-FRYING
2   TABLESPOONS DIJON MUSTARD
1   TABLESPOON VEGETABLE OIL
1   (1 LB. 10-OZ.) PKG. GREEN GIANT®
    CREATE A MEAL!® FROZEN OVEN
    ROASTED PARMESAN HERB

① Heat oven to 450°F. In small bowl, combine chicken and mustard; mix well.

② Pour oil into ungreased 13×9-inch baking pan. Stir in frozen vegetables and seasonings from packet; mix until evenly coated. Stir in mustard and chicken.

③ Bake at 450°F. for 20 minutes; stir. Bake an additional 10 to 15 minutes or until chicken is no longer pink.

Yield: 5 (1⅓-cup) servings

NUTRITION INFORMATION: SERVING SIZE: 1⅓ CUPS
CALORIES 270 (33% FROM FAT) • FAT 10 G (SAT. 3 G) • CHOLESTEROL 60 MG
SODIUM 1010 MG • CARBOHYDRATE 22 G • FIBER 4 G • PROTEIN 22 G

TIP

To substitute for precut poultry strips, slice boneless, skinless chicken breast into pieces about 2" x ½" x ½". Freeze the meat for 20 or 30 minutes to make slicing easier.

Bow Ties and Broccoli Alfredo

PREP TIME: 25 MINUTES (READY IN 55 MINUTES)

6 OZ. (3 CUPS) UNCOOKED BOW TIE
  PASTA (FARFALLE)
2 CUPS GREEN GIANT SELECT® 100%
  FROZEN BROCCOLI FLORETS
½ CUP SLICED PURCHASED ROASTED
  RED BELL PEPPERS
  (FROM 7.25-OZ. JAR)
½ TEASPOON DRIED BASIL LEAVES
⅛ TEASPOON PEPPER
1 (10-OZ.) CONTAINER REFRIGERATED
  ALFREDO SAUCE
2 TABLESPOONS SHREDDED FRESH
  PARMESAN CHEESE

1. Heat oven to 350°F. Grease 2-quart casserole. Cook pasta to desired doneness as directed on package, adding broccoli during last 2 to 3 minutes of cooking time. Drain.

2. In greased casserole, combine all ingredients except cheese; mix well. Cover.

3. Bake at 350°F. for 20 minutes. Uncover casserole; sprinkle with cheese. Bake, uncovered, an additional 5 to 10 minutes or until cheese is light golden brown.

Yield: 4 (1-cup) servings

NUTRITION INFORMATION: SERVING SIZE: 1 CUP
CALORIES 420 (52% FROM FAT) • FAT 24 G (SAT. 13 G) • CHOLESTEROL 50 MG
SODIUM 370 MG • CARBOHYDRATE 39 G • FIBER 2 G • PROTEIN 12 G

MAKING MEALS EASY

Broccoli Quiche

PREP TIME: 15 MINUTES (READY IN 1 HOUR 10 MINUTES)

CRUST

1 PILLSBURY REFRIGERATED PIE
    CRUST (FROM 15-OZ. PKG.)

FILLING

4 EGGS, SLIGHTLY BEATEN

1 CUP HALF-AND-HALF OR MILK

2 TABLESPOONS FINELY CHOPPED
    ONION

½ TEASPOON SALT

½ TEASPOON DRIED THYME LEAVES

1 (9-OZ.) PKG. GREEN GIANT® FROZEN
    CUT BROCCOLI, THAWED,
    WELL DRAINED

3 OZ. (¾ CUP) SHREDDED CHEDDAR
    CHEESE

3 OZ. (¾ CUP) SHREDDED MONTEREY
    JACK CHEESE

① Heat oven to 350°F. Prepare pie crust as directed on package for *one-crust filled pie* using 9-inch pie pan.

② In large bowl, combine eggs, half-and-half, onion, salt and thyme; mix well. Layer broccoli and cheeses in pie crust-lined pan. Pour egg mixture over top.

③ Bake at 350°F. for 40 to 50 minutes or until knife inserted near center comes out clean. Cool 5 minutes. Cut into wedges to serve.

Yield: 8 servings

NUTRITION INFORMATION: SERVING SIZE: ⅛ OF RECIPE
CALORIES 290 (62% FROM FAT) • FAT 20 G (SAT. 10 G) • CHOLESTEROL
145 MG • SODIUM 460 MG • CARBOHYDRATE 17 G • FIBER 1 G • PROTEIN 11 G

TIP

For variety, substitute a 9-ounce package Green Giant Frozen Asparagus Cuts in place of broccoli.

CASSEROLES

Chicken Divan

2 TABLESPOONS MARGARINE
   OR BUTTER

3 TABLESPOONS FLOUR

2 TEASPOONS CHICKEN-FLAVOR
   INSTANT BOUILLON

2 CUPS MILK

½ CUP MAYONNAISE OR SALAD
   DRESSING

1 TABLESPOON DIJON MUSTARD

1 (1-LB.) PKG. GREEN GIANT® FROZEN
   BROCCOLI SPEARS, THAWED,
   DRAINED

3 CUPS CUBED COOKED CHICKEN
   OR TURKEY

2 OZ. (½ CUP) SHREDDED CHEDDAR
   CHEESE

⅓ CUP UNSEASONED DRY BREAD
   CRUMBS

1 TABLESPOON MARGARINE OR BUTTER,
   MELTED

1. Heat oven to 350°F. Melt 2 tablespoons margarine in medium saucepan. Stir in flour and bouillon. Gradually stir in milk; cook until mixture boils and thickens, stirring constantly with wire whisk. Stir in mayonnaise and mustard until well blended.

2. Arrange broccoli spears in ungreased 12×8-inch (2-quart) baking dish. Top with chicken. Spoon sauce over chicken. Sprinkle with cheese.

3. In small bowl, combine bread crumbs and 1 tablespoon margarine; mix well. Sprinkle over top.

4. Bake at 350°F. for 30 minutes or until thoroughly heated.

Yield: 6 servings

NUTRITION INFORMATION: SERVING SIZE: ⅙ OF RECIPE
CALORIES 460 (61% FROM FAT) • FAT 31 G (SAT. 8 G) • CHOLESTEROL 90 MG
SODIUM 790 MG • FIBER 2 G • PROTEIN 29 G

Barbecue Chicken Cornmeal Bake

PREP TIME: 10 MINUTES (READY IN 45 MINUTES)

CRUST

1	CUP FLOUR
1	CUP YELLOW CORNMEAL
2	TEASPOONS BAKING POWDER
¼	TEASPOON SALT
1	CUP MILK
2	TABLESPOONS OIL
1	EGG

CHICKEN MIXTURE

1	(1 LB. 10-OZ.) PKG. GREEN GIANT® CREATE A MEAL!® OVEN ROASTED BARBECUE CHICKEN
2	TABLESPOONS OIL
1	LB. BONELESS SKINLESS CHICKEN BREAST HALVES, CUT INTO THIN STRIPS

① Heat oven to 400°F. Spray 13×9-inch pan with nonstick cooking spray.

② In medium bowl, combine flour, cornmeal, baking powder and salt; mix well. In small bowl, combine milk, 2 tablespoons oil and egg; blend well. Add to cornmeal mixture; stir just until combined. Spread batter in sprayed pan.

③ In large bowl, combine 2 tablespoons oil and vegetables. Add chicken; toss to mix. Sprinkle with seasonings from packet; toss to coat. Spoon over batter in pan.

④ Bake at 400°F. for 30 to 35 minutes or until chicken is no longer pink.

Yield: 6 servings

NUTRITION INFORMATION: SERVING SIZE: ⅙ OF RECIPE
CALORIES 470 (28% FROM FAT) • FAT 14 G (SAT. 3 G) • CHOLESTEROL 85 MG
SODIUM 1200 MG • CARBOHYDRATE 60 G • FIBER 5 G • PROTEIN 25 G

TIP

For added convenience, substitute one 8½-ounce package cornbread mix for the crust in this recipe. Simply prepare the mix as directed on the package.

Spinach Lasagna

PREP TIME: 40 MINUTES (READY IN 1 HOUR 30 MINUTES)

9	UNCOOKED LASAGNA NOODLES
2½	CUPS MILK
¼	CUP FLOUR
1	TEASPOON GARLIC SALT
2	(9-OZ.) PKG. GREEN GIANT® FROZEN SPINACH, THAWED, SQUEEZED TO DRAIN
1	CUP COTTAGE CHEESE
6	OZ. (1½ CUPS) SHREDDED MOZZARELLA CHEESE
¼	CUP GRATED PARMESAN CHEESE
	TOMATO WEDGES, IF DESIRED
	FRESH PARSLEY, IF DESIRED

① Cook lasagna noodles to desired doneness as directed on package. Drain; rinse with hot water.

② Meanwhile, heat oven to 350°F. In medium saucepan, combine milk, flour and garlic salt; blend well. Cook over medium heat, stirring constantly, until mixture boils and thickens. Reserve ½ cup white sauce for top layer of lasagna; stir spinach into remaining sauce.

③ In medium bowl, combine cottage cheese and mozzarella cheese. Spread ½ cup spinach sauce in bottom of ungreased 13×9-inch (3-quart) baking dish. Top with 3 lasagna noodles, half of cheese mixture and half of remaining spinach sauce; repeat layers. Top with last 3 noodles and reserved ½ cup white sauce. Sprinkle with Parmesan cheese.

④ Bake at 350°F. for 30 to 40 minutes or until thoroughly heated. Let stand 5 to 10 minutes before serving. Garnish individual servings with tomato wedges and basil leaves.

Yield: 6 servings

NUTRITION INFORMATION: SERVING SIZE: ⅙ OF RECIPE
CALORIES 340 (26% FROM FAT) • FAT 10 G (SAT. 6 G) • CHOLESTEROL 30 MG
SODIUM 940 MG • CARBOHYDRATE 37 G • FIBER 2 G • PROTEIN 25 G

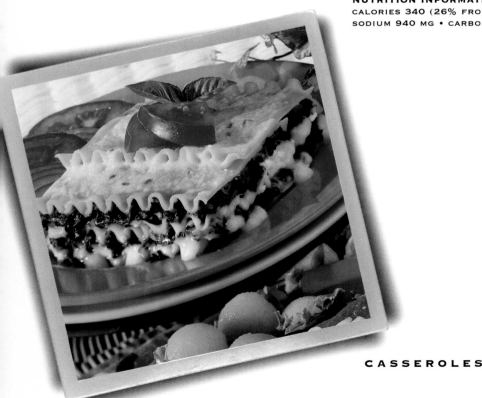

CASSEROLES

Swiss Spinach and Egg Au Gratin

PREP TIME: 20 MINUTES (READY IN 40 MINUTES)

1   EGG
1   (10-OZ.) PKG. GREEN GIANT®
    FROZEN CREAMED SPINACH
2   OZ. (½ CUP) SHREDDED SWISS
    CHEESE
2   TABLESPOONS UNSEASONED DRY
    BREAD CRUMBS
1   TABLESPOON MARGARINE OR BUTTER,
    MELTED
    PAPRIKA

1. Heat oven to 350°F. Grease 2-cup casserole or small loaf dish. Place egg in small saucepan; cover with cold water. Bring to a boil. Reduce heat; simmer about 15 minutes. Immediately drain; run cold water over egg to stop cooking. Peel egg; chop.

2. Cook spinach as directed on package. Spoon spinach into greased casserole; top with egg and cheese.

3. In small bowl, combine bread crumbs and margarine; mix well. Sprinkle over spinach mixture; sprinkle with paprika.

4. Bake at 350°F. for 15 to 20 minutes or until casserole is bubbly and topping is light golden brown.

Yield: 2 (1-cup) servings

NUTRITION INFORMATION: SERVING SIZE: 1 CUP
CALORIES 370 (57% FROM FAT) • FAT 23 G • (SAT. 10 G) • CHOLESTEROL 240 MG
SODIUM 930 MG • CARBOHYDRATE 19 G • FIBER 3 G • PROTEIN 21 G

Side Dishes

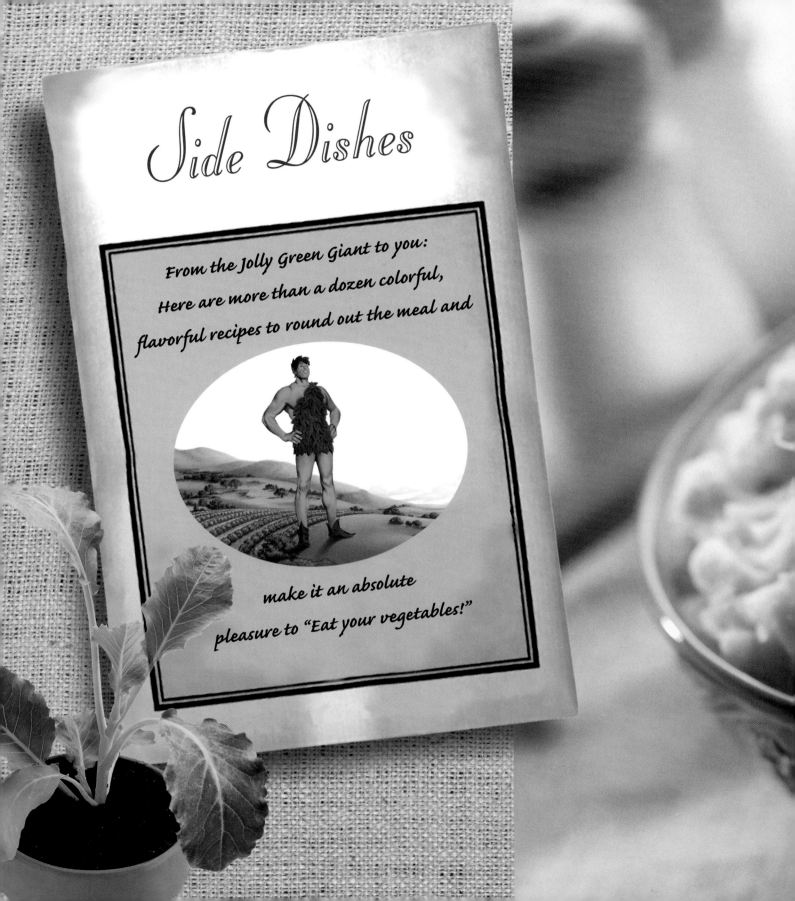

From the Jolly Green Giant to you:
Here are more than a dozen colorful,
flavorful recipes to round out the meal and

make it an absolute
pleasure to "Eat your vegetables!"

Easy Mashed Potatoes and Corn
(page 80)

Easy Mashed Potatoes and Corn

PICTURED ON PAGES 78–79

PREP TIME: 10 MINUTES

1 (11-OZ.) CAN GREEN GIANT® SUPER SWEET YELLOW AND WHITE CORN, UNDRAINED

2 CUPS MILK

3 TABLESPOONS MARGARINE OR BUTTER

½ TEASPOON SALT, IF DESIRED

⅛ TEASPOON PEPPER

2 CUPS HUNGRY JACK® MASHED POTATO FLAKES

½ CUP SOUR CREAM

2 TABLESPOONS SHREDDED FRESH PARMESAN CHEESE

2 TABLESPOONS REAL BACON BITS

1. In medium saucepan, combine corn, milk, margarine, salt and pepper; mix well. Cook over medium heat until mixture is hot and bubbly.

2. Remove from heat. Stir in potato flakes and sour cream until well blended. Sprinkle with Parmesan cheese and bacon bits.

Yield: 8 (½-cup) servings

NUTRITION INFORMATION: SERVING SIZE: ½ CUP
CALORIES 170 (35% FROM FAT) • FAT 7 G (SAT. 2 G) • CHOLESTEROL 10 MG
SODIUM 450 MG • CARBOHYDRATE 22 G • FIBER 2 G • PROTEIN 5 G

Creamy Parmesan Corn

PREP TIME: 10 MINUTES

1 (1-LB.) PKG. GREEN GIANT SELECT® FROZEN SHOEPEG WHITE CORN

½ CUP WHIPPING CREAM

2 TABLESPOONS GRATED PARMESAN CHEESE

DASH NUTMEG

1. Cook corn as directed on package. Drain.

2. Meanwhile, in medium saucepan, bring cream to a boil. Boil 2 minutes. Stir in Parmesan cheese until melted. Sprinkle with nutmeg. Pour over corn.

Yield: 5 (½-cup) servings

NUTRITION INFORMATION: SERVING SIZE: ½ CUP
CALORIES 190 (47% FROM FAT) • FAT 10 G (SAT. 6 G) • CHOLESTEROL 35 MG
SODIUM 50 MG • CARBOHYDRATE 21 G • FIBER 3 G • PROTEIN 4 G

Cheesy Peas and Potato Casserole

1 (9-OZ.) PKG. GREEN GIANT® LeSueur® FROZEN BABY SWEET PEAS

1½ CUPS WATER

3 TABLESPOONS BUTTER

1 (1.5-OZ.) PKG. FOUR-CHEESE TOSCANA SAUCE MIX

1 CUP MILK

2 CUPS HUNGRY JACK® MASHED POTATO FLAKES

¼ CUP GRATED PARMESAN AND ROMANO CHEESE BLEND

4 OZ. (1 CUP) SHREDDED SHARP CHEDDAR CHEESE

1 Cook peas as directed on package. Drain; keep warm.

2 Meanwhile, in medium saucepan, combine water, butter and sauce mix. Bring to a boil. Boil 1 minute, stirring constantly. Add milk. Remove from heat. Add potato flakes; with fork, beat well until potatoes are of desired consistency.*

3 In ungreased microwave-safe 9×5-inch (1½-quart) baking dish or 1½-quart casserole, layer half of the potatoes. Top with peas, Parmesan and Romano cheese blend and remaining half of potatoes. Sprinkle with Cheddar cheese. Microwave on HIGH for 2 to 4 minutes or until cheese is melted.

Yield: 6 (⅔-cup) servings

TIP: * FOR STIFFER POTATOES, STIR IN A FEW MORE POTATO FLAKES. FOR CREAMIER POTATOES, STIR IN A LITTLE MORE MILK.

NUTRITION INFORMATION:
SERVING SIZE: ⅔ CUP
CALORIES 320 (47% FROM FAT)
FAT 17 G (SAT. 10 G)
CHOLESTEROL 50 MG
SODIUM 790 MG
CARBOHYDRATE 29 G
FIBER 3 G • PROTEIN 13 G

Pea Pod Medley

PREP TIME: 10 MINUTES

1 CUP GREEN GIANT® FROZEN
    SWEET PEAS

1 CUP GREEN GIANT® FROZEN
    SUGAR SNAP PEAS

1 TABLESPOON MARGARINE OR BUTTER

1 GARLIC CLOVE, MINCED

1. In 1½-quart microwave-safe casserole, combine all ingredients; cover.

2. Microwave on HIGH for 5 to 6 minutes or until vegetables are thoroughly heated, stirring twice during cooking.

Yield: 4 (½-cup) servings

NUTRITION INFORMATION: SERVING SIZE: ½ CUP
CALORIES 60 (42% FROM FAT) • FAT 3 G (SAT. 1 G) • CHOLESTEROL 0 MG
SODIUM 70 MG • CARBOHYDRATE 6 G • FIBER 2 G • PROTEIN 2 G

Easy Risotto with Asparagus

PREP TIME: 40 MINUTES

1 TABLESPOON MARGARINE OR BUTTER

¼ CUP CHOPPED RED ONION

1 CUP UNCOOKED SHORT-GRAIN
    ARBORIO RICE, RINSED

2 (14½-OZ.) CANS READY-TO-SERVE
    VEGETABLE BROTH

½ CUP SLICED ROASTED RED BELL
    PEPPERS (FROM 7.25-OZ. JAR)

1 (9-OZ.) PKG. GREEN GIANT® FROZEN
    ASPARAGUS CUTS, THAWED,
    DRAINED

2 OZ. (½ CUP) SHREDDED FRESH
    PARMESAN CHEESE

1. Melt margarine in large skillet over medium-high heat. Add onion; cook and stir until tender. Stir in rice and 1 can of the broth. Bring to a boil. Reduce heat to medium; cook 8 to 10 minutes or until liquid is absorbed stirring frequently.

2. Add roasted peppers and asparagus; mix well. Cook an additional 15 to 17 minutes or until rice is tender, stirring frequently and adding additional broth ¼ cup at a time as necessary. (There may be a small amount of broth left.) Sprinkle with cheese.

Yield: 6 (¾-cup) servings

NUTRITION INFORMATION: SERVING SIZE: ¾ CUP
CALORIES 170 (26% FROM FAT) • FAT 5 G (SAT. 2 G) • CHOLESTEROL 5 MG
SODIUM 830 MG • CARBOHYDRATE 24 G FIBER 1 G • PROTEIN 6 G

Easy Risotto with Asparagus

Swiss Vegetable Casserole

PREP TIME: 20 MINUTES (READY IN 50 MINUTES)

1   (1-LB.) PKG. GREEN GIANT SELECT®
    FROZEN BROCCOLI, CARROTS
    AND CAULIFLOWER
2   TABLESPOONS MARGARINE OR
    BUTTER
6   GREEN ONIONS, CUT INTO ½-INCH
    PIECES (½ CUP)
2   TABLESPOONS FLOUR
¼   TEASPOON SALT
⅛   TEASPOON PEPPER
1½ CUPS MILK
4   OZ. (1 CUP) SHREDDED SWISS
    CHEESE
¼   CUP CRUSHED ROUND BUTTERY
    CRACKERS

1   Heat oven to 350°F. Grease 1 to 1½-quart casserole. Cook frozen vegetables as directed on package. Drain.

2   Meanwhile, melt margarine in medium saucepan over medium heat. Add onions; cook and stir 2 to 3 minutes or until tender.

3   Stir in flour, salt and pepper; mix well. Gradually add milk, stirring constantly. Cook and stir until mixture is bubbly and thickened. Remove from heat.

4   Add ¾ cup of the cheese; stir until melted. Stir in cooked vegetables. Spoon mixture into greased casserole. Sprinkle with crushed crackers and remaining ¼ cup cheese.

5   Bake at 350°F. for 25 to 30 minutes or until topping is golden brown and casserole is bubbly.

Yield: 8 (½-cup) servings

NUTRITION INFORMATION: SERVING SIZE: ½ CUP
CALORIES 140 (50% FROM FAT) • FAT 8 G • (SAT. 4 G) CHOLESTEROL 15 MG
SODIUM 200 MG • CARBOHYDRATE 10 G • FIBER 2 G • PROTEIN 7 G

SIDE DISHES

Uptown Broccoli

1 (1-LB.) PKG. GREEN GIANT SELECT®
FROZEN BROCCOLI SPEARS

1 TO 2 TABLESPOONS OLIVE OR
VEGETABLE OIL

¼ TO ½ CUP PINE NUTS

1 MEDIUM YELLOW OR RED BELL
PEPPER, CUT INTO THIN STRIPS

1 CUP PURCHASED RANCH SALAD
DRESSING

1 TABLESPOON CHOPPED FRESH DILL
OR 1 TEASPOON DRIED DILL WEED

1 TEASPOON PREPARED HORSERADISH

1 TEASPOON HONEY

¼ TEASPOON GARLIC POWDER

SHREDDED FRESH PARMESAN
CHEESE, IF DESIRED

1. Cook broccoli as directed on package. Drain; keep warm.

2. Meanwhile, heat oil in large skillet over medium heat until hot. Add pine nuts and bell pepper; cook and stir 5 minutes or until pine nuts are golden brown and bell pepper is crisp-tender. Drain; cover to keep warm.

3. In small saucepan, combine salad dressing, dill, horseradish, honey and garlic powder; mix well. Cook over medium heat for 2 minutes or until thoroughly heated, stirring constantly. DO NOT BOIL.

4. To serve, arrange broccoli spears on serving platter. Top with pine nuts and bell pepper. Spoon sauce over top. Garnish with cheese.

Yield: 6 servings

NUTRITION INFORMATION: SERVING SIZE: ⅙ OF RECIPE
CALORIES 370 (84% FROM FAT) • FAT 34 G (SAT. 6 G) • CHOLESTEROL 5 MG
SODIUM 400 MG • CARBOHYDRATE 10 G • FIBER 3 G • PROTEIN 5 G

Select Sweet Peas and Bacon

PREP TIME: 10 MINUTES

1 (1-LB.) PKG. GREEN GIANT SELECT®
    LeSueur® FROZEN BABY
    SWEET PEAS
3 SLICES BACON, CUT UP
¼ CUP CHOPPED ONION
1 TEASPOON FLOUR
¼ CUP CIDER VINEGAR
2 TABLESPOONS SUGAR

1. Cook peas as directed on package. Drain. Place in serving bowl; cover to keep warm.

2. Meanwhile, cook bacon and onion in medium skillet until bacon is crisp and onion is slightly browned. With slotted spoon, remove bacon and onion from skillet; set aside.

3. Stir flour into bacon drippings. Add vinegar and sugar; cook until bubbly and thickened, stirring constantly.

4. Pour sauce over peas; top with bacon and onion.

Yield: 5 (½-cup) servings

NUTRITION INFORMATION: SERVING SIZE: ½ CUP
CALORIES 170 (41% FROM FAT) • FAT 8 G (SAT. 3 G) • CHOLESTEROL 10 MG
SODIUM 270 MG • CARBOHYDRATE 19 G • FIBER 4 G • PROTEIN 6 G

Southwestern Corn

PREP TIME: 10 MINUTES

1 (1-LB.) PKG. GREEN GIANT SELECT®
    GOLD AND WHITE CORN
½ CUP DICED FRESH RED AND/OR
    GREEN BELL PEPPER OR ROASTED
    RED BELL PEPPERS
1 TEASPOON CUMIN
½ TEASPOON GARLIC SALT
½ TEASPOON GRATED LIME PEEL

1. Cook corn as directed on package. Drain; return corn to saucepan.

2. Add all remaining ingredients; mix well. Stir over low heat for 1 to 2 minutes or until thoroughly heated.

Yield: 6 (½-cup) servings

NUTRITION INFORMATION: SERVING SIZE: ½ CUP
CALORIES 70 (14% FROM FAT) • FAT 1 G (SAT. 0 G) • CHOLESTEROL 0 MG
SODIUM 160 MG • CARBOHYDRATE 12 G • FIBER 2 G • PROTEIN 2 G

Top: Select Sweet Peas and Bacon
Bottom: Southwestern Corn

Easy Vegetable Sauces

Pair our sauces with these cooked vegetables
or devise your own imaginative duos.

Tangy Lemon Sauce

Asparagus, sugar snap peas, green beans

Orange Browned Butter Sauce

Carrots, broccoli, cauliflower, sugar snap peas

Chive Cheese Sauce

Cauliflower, broccoli, boiled potatoes

Hot Bacon and Onion Sauce

Potatoes, broccoli, green beans, peas

Easy Mushroom Sauce

Mashed potatoes, green beans, peas

Maple Pecan Sauce

Sweet potatoes, cauliflower, winter squash, carrots

Asian Ginger Glaze

Asparagus, broccoli, carrots, green beans

Tangy Lemon Sauce

¼ CUP REGULAR, LIGHT OR FAT-FREE
     MAYONNAISE
¼ CUP SOUR CREAM
2 TABLESPOONS BUTTER, MELTED
1 TEASPOON GRATED LEMON PEEL, IF
     DESIRED
2 TEASPOONS LEMON JUICE

(1) In small saucepan, combine all ingredients; mix well. Heat over low heat until warm, stirring constantly. Or, mix in small microwave-safe cup or dish; heat in microwave for 30-second increments until warm. (Watch carefully; it will not take long.)

Yield: Enough for 6 (½-cup) servings of hot cooked vegetables

NUTRITION INFORMATION: SERVING SIZE: ⅙ OF RECIPE
CALORIES 120 (100% FROM FAT) • FAT 13 G (SAT. 5 G) • CHOLESTEROL 20 MG
SODIUM 95 MG • CARBOHYDRATE 1 G • FIBER 0 G • PROTEIN 0 G

Orange Browned Butter Sauce

⅓ CUP BUTTER
1 TEASPOON GRATED ORANGE PEEL
½ TEASPOON GRATED GINGERROOT
2 TABLESPOONS ORANGE JUICE

(1) In small saucepan, cook butter over medium-high heat until golden brown; immediately remove from heat. Add orange peel, gingerroot and orange juice; mix well.

Yield: Enough for 8 (½-cup) servings of hot cooked vegetables

NUTRITION INFORMATION: SERVING SIZE: ⅛ CUP
CALORIES 70 (100% FROM FAT) • FAT 8 G (SAT. 5 G) • CHOLESTEROL 20 MG
SODIUM 80 MG • CARBOHYDRATE 1 G • FIBER 0 G • PROTEIN 0 G

Chive Cheese Sauce

PREP TIME: 5 MINUTES

½ CUP LIGHT PASTEURIZED PROCESS
   CHEESE PRODUCT

2 TABLESPOONS CHOPPED FRESH
   CHIVES

¼ TEASPOON DRY MUSTARD

2 TABLESPOONS SKIM MILK

1. In small saucepan, combine all ingredients. Cook and stir over medium heat until cheese is melted and mixture is smooth.

Yield: Enough for 10 (½-cup) servings of hot cooked vegetables

TIP: * WHEN TIME IS SHORT, THIS SIMPLE CHEESE SAUCE IS READY IN A FLASH. REFRIGERATE LEFTOVER SAUCE AND REHEAT IT IN THE MICROWAVE.

NUTRITION INFORMATION: SERVING SIZE: 1/10 OF RECIPE
CALORIES 30 (33% FROM FAT) • FAT 1 G (SAT. 1 G) • CHOLESTEROL 5 MG
SODIUM 190 MG • CARBOHYDRATE 2 G • FIBER 0 G • PROTEIN 3 G

Hot Bacon and Onion Sauce

PREP TIME: 15 MINUTES

2 SLICES BACON, CUT INTO SMALL
   PIECES

1 SMALL ONION, HALVED, THINLY
   SLICED

¼ CUP FIRMLY PACKED BROWN SUGAR

2 TEASPOONS FLOUR

⅛ TEASPOON PEPPER

⅓ CUP CIDER VINEGAR

⅓ CUP WATER

1. In medium saucepan over medium heat, cook bacon just until it begins to brown.

2. Add onion; cook 3 to 5 minutes or until onion is tender, stirring frequently.

3. Stir in all remaining ingredients. Cook until bubbly, stirring frequently.

Yield: Enough for 8 (½-cup) servings of hot cooked vegetables

NUTRITION INFORMATION:
SERVING SIZE: ⅛ OF RECIPE
CALORIES 70 (36% FROM FAT)
FAT 3 G (SAT. 1 G)
CHOLESTEROL 4 MG
SODIUM 45 MG
CARBOHYDRATE 9 G
FIBER 0 G
PROTEIN 1 G

Easy Mushroom Sauce

PREP TIME: 15 MINUTES

1 TABLESPOON MARGARINE OR BUTTER

2 TABLESPOONS CHOPPED ONION

1 (4-OZ.) CAN GREEN GIANT®
    MUSHROOM PIECES AND STEMS,
    DRAINED, COARSELY CHOPPED

½ CUP PURCHASED GRAVY FOR PORK

¼ CUP WATER

¼ TEASPOON DRIED MARJORAM LEAVES,
    IF DESIRED

2 TABLESPOONS CHOPPED FRESH
    PARSLEY

(1) Melt margarine in medium nonstick saucepan over medium heat. Add onion; cook and stir 2 minutes.

(2) Add mushrooms; cook 4 minutes, stirring occasionally.

(3) Add gravy, water and marjoram; mix well. Bring to a boil. Reduce heat; simmer 5 minutes. Stir in parsley.

Yield: Enough for 6 (½-cup) servings of hot cooked vegetables

NUTRITION INFORMATION: SERVING SIZE: ⅙ OF RECIPE
CALORIES 35 (57% FROM FAT) • FAT 2 G (SAT. 0 G) • CHOLESTEROL 0 MG
SODIUM 190 MG • CARBOHYDRATE 3 G • FIBER 1 G • PROTEIN 1 G

MAKING MEALS EASY

Maple Pecan Sauce

PREP TIME: 20 MINUTES

¼ CUP FINELY CHOPPED PECANS
1 TABLESPOON FINELY CHOPPED ONION
¼ CUP CHICKEN BROTH
¾ CUP MAPLE-FLAVORED SYRUP

(1) Place pecans in small nonstick saucepan; stir over medium-high heat for 3 to 5 minutes or until lightly browned. Remove pecans from saucepan; set aside.

(2) In same saucepan, combine onion and broth. Bring to a boil. Cook 3 minutes or until onion is tender.

(3) Stir in syrup; return to a boil. Boil 5 minutes, stirring occasionally. Stir in pecans.

Yield: Enough for 6 (½-cup) servings of hot cooked vegetables

NUTRITION INFORMATION: SERVING SIZE: ⅙ OF RECIPE
CALORIES 140 (18% FROM FAT) • FAT 3 G (SAT. 0 G)
CHOLESTEROL 0 MG • SODIUM 80 MG • CARBOHYDRATE 27 G
FIBER 1 G • PROTEIN 1 G

Asian Ginger Glaze

PREP TIME: 15 MINUTES

1 TEASPOON SESAME SEED, IF DESIRED
¾ CUP CHICKEN BROTH
2 TABLESPOONS FROZEN ORANGE JUICE
   CONCENTRATE
1 TABLESPOON SOY SAUCE
2 TEASPOONS CORNSTARCH
½ TEASPOON GRATED GINGERROOT OR
   ⅛ TEASPOON GINGER
¼ TEASPOON GARLIC POWDER

(1) Place sesame seed in small saucepan; stir over medium-high heat for 3 to 5 minutes or until toasted. Remove sesame seed from saucepan; set aside.

(2) In same saucepan, combine all remaining ingredients; stir until well blended. Bring to a boil, stirring constantly. Boil 1 minute or until thickened and clear, stirring constantly. Remove from heat; stir in sesame seed.

Yield: Enough for 6 (½-cup) servings of hot cooked vegetables

NUTRITION INFORMATION: SERVING SIZE: ⅙ OF RECIPE
CALORIES 20 (0% FROM FAT) • FAT 0 G (SAT. 0 G) • CHOLESTEROL 0 MG
SODIUM 270 MG • CARBOHYDRATE 4 G • FIBER 0 G • PROTEIN 1 G

MAKING MEALS EASY

HOW TO USE OUR NUTRITION INFORMATION

T he key to healthy eating is a varied diet including many fruits, vegetables and grains. The detailed nutrition information in Classic® Cookbooks can help you estimate the contribution of specific recipes in your overall menu plan. At the end of each recipe, we list the calories per serving as well as the amount of fat, cholesterol, sodium, carbohydrate, dietary fiber and protein.

- If you are following a medically prescribed diet, consult your physician or registered dietitian about this nutrition information.

HOW TO CALCULATE NUTRITION INFORMATION:

To determine a serving size for calculating nutrients for a recipe, we base our analysis on a single unit (for example, 1 cookie) or a specific amount (1 cup).

Other considerations for calculating nutrition information are:

- The first ingredient mentioned when the recipe gives options—for example, if "butter or margarine" is listed, butter would be calculated
- The larger amount of an ingredient when there's a range
- Garnishing or "if desired" ingredients when included in the ingredient list
- The estimated amount of marinade or frying oil absorbed during preparation

Our Experts Behind the Scenes:

Our team of professionals, including registered dietitians and home economists, is dedicated to delivering comprehensive nutrition information to make your job of planning nutritious menus for you and your family just a little easier. Current information from the USDA and food manufacturers' labels are used to provide up-to-date nutrient values.

Tailoring Your Daily Diet

The chart below outlines some average daily nutritional needs for moderately active adults.

Since your sex, age, size and activity level all affect dietary considerations, your requirements may deviate from those shown here.

What You Need Daily	Women Age: 25–50	Women Over 50	Men 25–50
Calories	2200	1900	2900
Total Fat	73 g or less	63	97
Saturated Fat	24 g or less	21	32
Cholesterol	300 mg or less	300	300
Sodium	2400 mg	2400	2400
Calcium	800 mg	800	800
Iron	15 mg	10	10

(Note: Although individual needs vary, a 2000-calorie diet is used as the reference diet on packaging because it approximates average daily requirements and provides a round number for easier calculating.)